D0869600

IBM

الصالون العصري
Salon Moderne
LORD
LORD

مكتبة
اخوان الصفا وخلان الوفا
LIBRARIE DES AMIS DES LETTRES

ICC

الهيئة العامة للتأمين الصحى
فرع شمال غرب الدلتا
عيادة الحضرية

CONTENTS

ALEXANDRIA
PAST, PRESENT AND FUTURE

Jean-Yves Empereur

ΛΟΣ
ΙΕΙ

‘The architects had begun to chalk in the lines of the enclosure when the supply of chalk ran out; the king was arriving, so the stewards of the works gave the architects some of the barley meal for the workmen’s food, and it was with this meal that a good number of the lines of the roads were now marked out, and the occurrence was then interpreted, it is said, as a good omen.’

Strabo (64/63 BC–AD 21), *Geography*, XVII, 1, 6

CHAPTER 1
ANCIENT ALEXANDRIA

The city’s founder, Alexander the Great, is depicted on this coin (right) wearing the horns of Ammon, the ram-god of the oasis of Siwa who declared himself his father. Queen Berenice II (opposite) wears on her head the prow of a ship, probably as a token of her husband Ptolemy III’s victory in a naval battle. This late 3rd-century BC mosaic was long thought to be a personification of the city of Alexandria.

In 332 BC, after defeating the Persians, Alexander III of Macedonia (356–323 BC) turned south towards Egypt. There he overthrew the Achaemenid satrap Mazaces and entered Memphis, the old pharaonic capital. Egypt became part of the Hellenic world. As the country was reorganized there was an inevitable shift in focus to the Mediterranean.

Choice of site

What were the reasons that made Alexander the Great choose this particular site for the future Alexandria? The Macedonian ruler's overall purpose was to bring Egypt closer to the Greek world, and he wanted to found a new port that would not be affected by the Nile floods. His choice fell on a spot lying on a rocky spit of land that was as close as practicable to the Nile. It had the added advantage of being associated with an island already familiar to the Greeks, ever since the poet Homer had used it as the setting for an episode of the *Odyssey*. Strabo, in the first century BC, refers to an Egyptian city predating the foundation of Alexandria called Rhakotis. In fact, 'Rhakotis' (*Raqed* in Egyptian, literally 'building site') was what the Egyptian workmen called the city, because they refused to use its founder's name.

Alexandria was built between the sea and a lake, west of the mouth of the Canopic branch of the Nile, visible at the left (we are looking from the north-west). In the far distance, at the apex of the Delta, lies Memphis. Lake Mareotis (now Mariout) was created by the formation of an offshore bar that closed the mouth of the former gulf. More like an inland sea than a lake, extending 100 km (60 miles) east to west, it was linked to the Nile by canals that served the vineyards and towns along its banks. According to Strabo, the lakeside ports were even busier than those on Alexandria's maritime coast.

The city of Alexandria

When the city was founded in 331 BC, Alexander and his architect Dinocrates of Rhodes had already roughly planned its layout, on a gigantic scale that was greatly to impress the ancient world. Alexander wanted his city to be a 'megalopolis', with walls stretching endlessly into the distance (they were over 15 km [10 miles] in circumference) and streets of exceptional width – 30 m [100 feet] in the case of the two main streets and 15 m [50 feet] for the rest – exceeding anything that had previously been seen. Applying Aristotle's principles for planning the ideal city, a rectangular grid of streets was designed, orientated in such a way as to profit from the sea breezes, or conversely to provide shelter from the wind. Provision was also made for the Heptastadion, a mole 7 *stadia* in length (by the standard Alexandrian measure, 7 × 167 m [23 × 548 feet]), linking the island of Pharos to the mainland, and thereby creating two large ports that offered shelter from the north winds on this low-lying and hazardous coast.

Many portraits of Alexander have been discovered in Alexandria, among them this granite head from the 1st century BC. It is typical of the statues of the city's heroic founder that graced its public spaces, temples and private houses.

All that remains of Alexandria's ancient walls is a small section in the Shallalat Gardens near the eastern gate. Whether it is Hellenistic or Roman is unknown.

The Alexandrians drank Nile water. Unable to rely on the rainfall, which varied from year to year, the city was linked by a canal to the Canopic branch of the Nile. In late summer the floodwater invaded the canal, and filled the many subterranean cisterns (left, that of el-Nabi). Public health and prosperity depended on the system being well maintained.

It was Ptolemy I (below, with his wife Berenice I) who moved the capital of Egypt from Memphis to Alexandria. There he embarked on an ambitious scheme of public works, building the Pharos, the Great Library, the Mouseion and the Tomb of Alexander the Great. His son, Ptolemy II, continued the programme.

Infrastructure

The site was less than 30 km (20 miles) from the mouth of the Canopic branch of the Nile, with which the Greeks were familiar because they already had a trading post at Naucratis 70 km (50 miles) into the Delta, founded in the 7th century BC in cooperation with the Pharaoh Amasis. The Nile could also be reached by means of canals from Lake Mareotis, which lay to the south of the city-in-the-making. Another canal was dug soon afterwards which linked the city to the

Canopic branch of the Nile, ensuring a constant supply of fresh water.

This particular canal was used to replenish the cisterns that were being built in ever-increasing numbers under the city. They were filled once a year, when the Nile flood reached Alexandria in August/September. Travellers from earlier centuries have described the festival of the *khalig* ('canal') which, as in Cairo, was held to mark the opening of secondary canals running from south to north. As these became flooded in their turn, the flow of water was directed into the cisterns. Using this method water could be stored for a whole year, and brought to the surface when it was needed by means of a *saqiya*, or wheel equipped with buckets, that was turned by draught animals.

A new capital

Alexander died in Babylon in 323 BC, never having seen the city whose foundations he had laid eight years before. His generals disputed the succession among themselves and eventually shared out the remnants of the empire. Egypt fell to Ptolemy in 319 BC, and he proclaimed himself king in 305 BC. This seasoned campaigner, a childhood friend of Alexander, was to prove an outstanding administrator. The dynasty he founded held sway over Egypt's destiny until 30 BC, the date of Cleopatra's death and of the annexation of Egypt by Rome.

Ptolemy was at first undecided over his choice of capital and for a few years it seems that Memphis, the pharaonic capital and coronation city, fulfilled that function. His ultimate preference was however for the new city on the northern coast, Alexandria, which in the event was to remain the seat of government for a thousand years, until the Arab conquest of AD 640. The new ruler, taking the name of Soter ('saviour'), set about embellishing the city with monuments worthy of Alexander's grand design.

On the Stela of the Satrap (311 BC) Ptolemy I, then still satrap of Egypt, set out his policies on religion for the Egyptian priesthood. For the first time the name of Alexandria appears in Egyptian form: 'Wall of the King of Upper and Lower Egypt, of the Son of Re, Alexander.' This attempt to produce an official translation came to nothing: the Egyptians refused to call the city by its founder's name and called it instead by the word meaning 'building site', *Raqed*.

The Tomb of Alexander the Great

To confirm the status of the new city, Ptolemy I built a tomb for Alexander the Great in the vicinity of the palace quarter. He had managed to seize the conqueror's corpse by force of arms as it was being transported from Babylon to Macedonia, and his plan was to preserve it as a relic in order to ensure the city's prosperity. Indeed, as we know from ancient sources, the Tomb was to become one of the most famous monuments of antiquity. Octavian (the future Augustus; 63 BC–AD 14), we are told, decorated the mummy with a gold crown, and in the process broke its nose. There are records of visits by Roman emperors right up to Caracalla, at the start of the 3rd century AD. Then, silence.

It is probable that, like the Library, the Tomb or Soma (literally 'the body') fell victim to the violent wars into which Alexandria was plunged during the second half of the 3rd century. When, at the end of the following century, St John Chrysostom asked the pagans of Alexandria 'Where, then, is Alexander's Tomb?', all knowledge of its location had disappeared from the collective memory.

This alabaster structure was found in the Latin cemeteries in 1907 and restored in 1936 by Achille Adriani, the last Italian director of the Greco-Roman Museum, who dated it to the late 4th century BC, and identified it as the antechamber to the Tomb of Alexander. New excavations are being carried out in the hope of finding more remains of the royal necropolis, even the Tomb of Alexander itself.

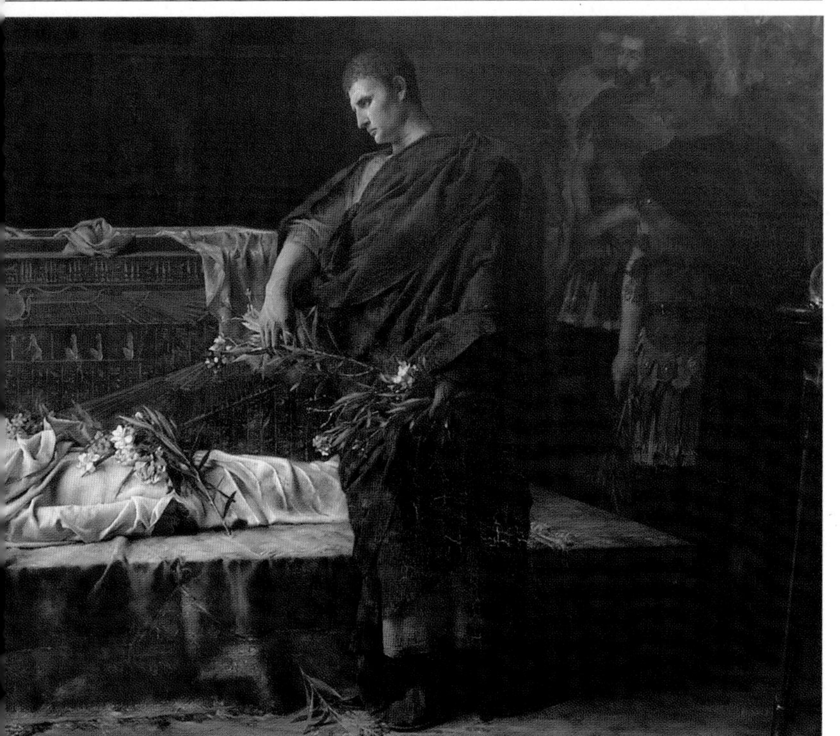

In his description of Alexandria in 25 BC, Strabo tells us that the Soma lay within the precinct of the royal palaces. This gave rise to a theory as to the Tomb's location that appears to be corroborated by a passage in *The Adventures of Leucippe and Cleitophon*, a novel by Achilles Tatius (2nd century AD). According to this, the royal necropolis stood at the corner of the two main streets of the city – R1, which led from the palace down to the royal port on Lake Mareotis, and L1, now known as the Canopic Way.

But was the Tomb really within the heart of the palace quarter, or at its edge? It is not inconceivable that archaeologists may one day happen on Alexander's Tomb – but if they did, would they necessarily recognize it, given its likely state of dilapidation?

After his victory over Cleopatra and Mark Antony in the naval battle of Actium in 31 BC, Octavian captured Alexandria. Entering Alexander's Tomb, he had the body removed from its sarcophagus so that he could place a crown on the hero's head.

In this painting, Alexandria lies between the sea to the north (top) and Lake Mareotis to the south. To the east of the small island of Pharos stands the Lighthouse, itself known as the Pharos. A causeway/bridge called the Heptastadion links the island to the mainland, creating two ports: to the west the 'Eunostos' or 'port of good return', and to the east the 'Megas Limen', or 'great port'. Along the southern coast are the lakeside ports. Outside the city walls, 15 km (10 miles) in extent, are the necropolises and, to the south, a canal linked to the Nile. Clearly visible are the two main streets, which meet at a crossroads.

A city of palaces

Alexandria was vast, extending 5 km (3 miles) from east to west within the walls and 2–3 km (1–2 miles) from north to south, depending on the irregularities of the coastline and lake shore. The city was divided into administrative zones: from texts we know the numbers allocated to some of these (there were at least five), but we have no precise indication as to their location. The same is true for many of the monuments of which we have descriptions, notably by Strabo: it is impossible to find any trace of them on the ground, or even to situate them within the topography of the ancient city. It is as though they remained suspended over a map on which they could never be set down.

The division into quarters perfectly reflects the city's dual role – as both a political centre and a royal residence. One whole district was given over to the royal palaces. Here, where he lived, Ptolemy sited his administrative headquarters, and here his successors went on living. Each of those successors in turn added a new palace to the complex, until it must have formed a sort of Forbidden City within the larger city, if we can believe Strabo's description. This is what he wrote after he had visited Alexandria: 'The city contains some splendid parks and the royal buildings, which occupy a quarter if not

The Canopic Way (opposite) ran from the Gate of the Sun in the east to the Gate of the Moon 5 km (3 miles) to the west. Strabo tells us it was 30 m (100 feet) wide, and Achilles Tatius says it was lined with colonnades. When those were built is unknown; Alexandria may have been the first city to have the arcaded streets so characteristic of the Roman towns of the eastern Mediterranean.

Housing for the first generation of Alexandrians: a dining room paved with a pebble mosaic (above), as in Alexander's native land of Macedonia, and a two-storeyed house, its loggia partly closed off by curtains, depicted in a lantern (left).

a third of the total area, for each of the kings, desirous in his turn of embellishing the public buildings with some new ornament, was no less desirous of adding, at his own expense, a further residence to those already in existence. . . . All these buildings form a continuous structure, [comprising] themselves, the port, and even those that lie beyond the port. The Mouseion too forms part of the royal buildings.' Ptolemy I commissioned most of the monuments that before long graced the new city: the Pharos, the Library and adjacent Mouseion, Alexander's Tomb, and the principal temples.

Depending on where their statues were to be displayed, the Ptolemies were depicted either in the guise of Hellenistic kings or with pharaonic attributes, as in this head of Ptolemy IV. They officially assumed the title of pharaoh in the old capital of Memphis.

Home of the gods

To establish lasting dominion over Egypt, the dynasty of the Lagides (from the name of Ptolemy's father, Lagus, or 'hare') needed to prove to the Greeks that they were the true heirs of Alexander, and to the Egyptians, and the priests in particular, that they were the true descendants of the ancient pharaohs.

Ptolemy I not only built temples in Alexandria dedicated to the Egyptian divinities – written sources refer to a dozen or so temples to Isis – but also founded entirely new cults. He can certainly be credited with the invention of a deity called Sarapis. In Memphis the god Apis, whose earthly form was that of a bull, had long been worshipped. Ptolemy took up this cult and adapted it to suit the Greeks, who were disinclined to worship a god in zoomorphic form – the 5th-century BC historian Herodotus had already expressed his incomprehension at this aspect of pharaonic religion – by giving him

This black basalt statue of the bull Apis is life-size. It was discovered intact a century ago during excavations at the Sarapeum. An inscription in Greek proclaims that it was dedicated by the Emperor Hadrian (a great lover of Egypt) on one of his visits to Alexandria, around AD 130.

the anthropomorphic features of a bearded Zeus, distinguished by ringlets on his forehead. Sarapis combined the powers of the ruler of Olympus, of Asclepius, god of healing, and of Hades, lord of the underworld.

Sarapis formed a new triad with Isis, the sister-wife of Osiris, and their son Harpocrates ('Horus the child'). The cult of these healing gods became extraordinarily popular, and spread rapidly and steadily beyond the walls of Alexandria. *Sarapeia*, or temples of Sarapis, were founded throughout the Mediterranean area, and in the 1st century AD Sarapis joined the pantheon of gods worshipped on the Capitol.

The Sarapeum was the most prominent of Alexandria's temples, standing as it did on one of the city's few hills (grandly known, despite its modest proportions, as the Acropolis). A flight of one hundred steps led up the hill to the 'Daughter Library' (so called because it contained copies of works of which the originals were in the Great Library), a Nilometer, subterranean chambers used for the cult of the bull god, and a temple which was extended under Ptolemy II, Ptolemy IV and Hadrian. A late 4th-century writer, Rufinus, provides a relatively detailed account of the ritual performed when the statue of Sarapis was brought out to receive the 'Kiss of the Sun', or in other words to be recharged with divine energy.

Sarapis was one of the great divinities of Hellenistic Egypt. He appeared to his Greek adherents in anthropomorphic form, as in this monumental statue made of sycamore wood. Apart from the characteristic five locks of hair on his forehead, the god was originally distinguished by the *calathos* or *modius*, a headdress shaped like a grain measure.

In the catacombs of Kom es-Shoqafa, the main chapel is decorated with reliefs from the end of the 1st century AD. Here, three Egyptian gods, Anubis, Thoth and Horus, preside over the mummification of Osiris. The sarcophagus is decorated in Greek style with two heads of satyrs, companions of Dionysus.

Another example of Alexandrian religious synthesis is this oil lamp in the shape of an Egyptian temple (2nd century BC). Its pediment bears a solar disk, its cornice is ornamented with *uraei* (rearing cobras), and its capitals are heads of Hathor. Inside, however, is a statue of Aphrodite bathing.

This involved sophisticated processes, including the use of magnets, of which there is evidence in other Alexandrian shrines as well. The miracle commanded the admiration of the faithful, and contributed greatly to the popularity of Sarapis.

Another very popular Alexandrian deity was Agathos Daimon – the good genius – who appeared in the form of a snake. He was associated with a pharaonic divinity who also adopted the guise of a serpent, and was worshipped as a guarantor of prosperity, in memory of the snakes that left the foundations of the new city, an event that was regarded by the soothsayers as a good omen. Agathos Daimon

was specially celebrated on the anniversary of the city's foundation. Greek and Egyptian gods lived happily side by side in Alexandria. Their coexistence was made easier still by the practice of the Greeks who, following the example of Herodotus, saw parallels between the two sets of divinities. Hermes, for instance, became identified with Thoth, Aphrodite with Hathor, and so on. Indeed, the longer the Greeks remained in Egypt, the more elements they took over from Egyptian religion. The dead themselves tell the tale, thanks to recent rescue excavations at the Necropolis. Whereas during the 4th and 3rd centuries BC the Alexandrians followed Greek burial customs, and practised burial and cremation, towards the end of the Ptolemaic period a section of the population adopted the Egyptian practice of mummification. This represented a complete revolution in attitudes. Alexandrians had hitherto expected after death to go to the Greek Hades, a pale replica of the world of the living, where the dead spent their time regretting their earthly existence; but now they preserved the body with obsessive care in preparation for resurrection like that of Osiris. Thus a distinctively Alexandrian religious synthesis came into being, one that combined Greek and Egyptian practices. We have good evidence for this, of which some of the most remarkable appears in relief sculptures in the catacombs of Kom es-Shoqafa: here we see the mummification of the dead person by Anubis, a sarcophagus with emblems of Dionysus, and Agathos Daimon wearing the *pschent*, or double crown of the pharaohs.

The ibis, emblem of Thoth, holds the caduceus or staff of Hermes on this 2nd-century BC marble plaque (left), dedicated to Isis, Sarapis and Hermes (instead of Thoth). The deity Agathos Daimon (below) was a reminder of the link between snakes and the city's prosperity; here he appears with the pharaonic double crown.

A Roman mosaic of the 2nd century AD shows a scene somewhere in the Nile region, probably on the shore of Lake Mareotis: a banquet is taking place in the shade of a canopy, and a dancer performs before the reclining diners.

These terracotta 'Tanagra' figurines were found in graves – hence their exceptional state of preservation and the freshness of their colouring.

The Alexandrians

The religious synthesis that we have been considering reflected the city's ethnic diversity: Egyptians, Greeks, Jews, Phoenicians, Nabateans, Arabs and Indians – all the races in the world rubbed shoulders on the streets of Alexandria. But we should not therefore conclude that it was a cosmopolitan place in which all communities enjoyed similar privileges, for in fact the population of Alexandria was subject to a strict hierarchy.

How did one become an Alexandrian? The preconditions for citizenship were stringent, as in any other Greek city. Both your father and your mother had to be Alexandrian citizens. On reaching adolescence, your claim to citizenship was examined, and the lists were posted on the tribune in the precinct of the great gymnasium. These lists determined your admission to a tribe, your entrance to the Greek education system in one of the city's gymnasia, your eligibility for service in the army, and many other things beside.

Below this first tier, which formed an exclusive group, was a second tier composed of 'Hellenes',

that is Greeks from other cities, from settlements on the mainland, on the islands, and in Asia Minor. They were not Alexandrian citizens. Also included in this second category were the Jews, who had formed a sizeable minority within the city since Ptolemy I first enlisted them to serve in his army. These Hellenized and Greek-speaking Jews had often lost their ability to understand Hebrew and Aramaic, and Greek translations of the scriptures had to be made for them. Thracians, Carians and others also figured in the second category.

‘GORGO: Praxinoa . . . get your dress and cloak. Let's go to the royal palace, home of the wealthy Ptolemy; we shall see Adonis. I heard the queen was planning something special. . . . Praxinoa, that pleated dress really suits you. Tell me, how much was the cloth?
PRAXINOA: Don't ask, Gorgo! Two silver minas at least. And having it made up! That just about finished me off. . . . (*To her slave Eunoa*) Bring me my cloak and my hat. Drape it just so. . . . Let's go.’

Theocritus, *The Ladies of Syracuse*, *c.* 270 BC

The third and largest category comprised the many Egyptians living in Alexandria – probably far too many at times in the eyes of the Greeks, since texts record mass expulsions which were designed to force the Egyptians out of the city and back to cultivate the land in the Delta.

Yet the Greeks needed the Egyptians, not only for construction work but in the functioning of the administration, where they were essential cogs in the machine transmitting the orders of the Greek rulers to the indigenous population. These administrators and translators, and members of the priesthood, constituted a homogeneous force that needed to be treated carefully, with a balance being struck between imposed taxation and respect for the age-old privileges of the temples.

A bronze head of a young black woman. Nubians were often brought to Alexandria as slaves.

Young Alexandrians received an excellent education, which included the study of Greek authors such as Homer and the tragic playwrights. This scene of Greek-style education is set in a gymnasium in Alexandria, against the background of a portico with Corinthian capitals. The schoolmaster is disciplining one of the pupils. Another pupil scrapes himself with a strigil, while a third, on the right, is practising running, holding a torch in his hand (terracotta lamp, 2nd century BC).

They found ways of coming to terms with the power of the Ptolemies, and some indeed rose to occupy positions of influence at court and became Hellenized themselves, at least to outward appearances.

Contemporary writers suggest that the Alexandrian populace had the reputation of being irreverent, rebellious trouble-makers. Certainly the proximity of the palaces sometimes led them to intervene directly in affairs of state. Achilles Tatius conveys the effect of this teeming mass of people. When his novel's hero Cleitophon disembarks in Alexandria for the first time, he is unrestrained in his admiration: 'When I contemplated the city, I thought there could never be enough inhabitants to fill it entirely; but when I looked at the inhabitants, I asked myself in amazement if there could ever be a city capable of containing them.'

The owner of a hypogeum in Kom es-Shoqafa is represented by a statue placed in a naos, or cell, hollowed from the rock. He is standing in the Egyptian manner, arms against his sides, and wears a simple loincloth, but his face is individualized, with prominent cheekbones and a mass of curly hair. This is a rich Alexandrian of the late 1st century AD.

The final resting place

In the suburbs beyond the walls lie vast cemeteries. To the west is the Necropolis, or 'city of the dead' – a term coined by Strabo specifically for the Alexandrian cemetery, to convey his amazement at its scale, as immense as the city of the living. The diverse nature of the tombs reflects differences in social class. In some places the skeletons are buried directly in the ground; in others they are in hypogea (literally 'under the earth'), which link up to form underground mazes, with hundreds of body-size recesses hollowed out of the soft rock of the Alexandrian subsoil. Here we can see a funerary bed richly painted with flowers and geometric

The cemeteries of Alexandria lie beyond the city walls; they cover vast areas, and are among the most impressive in the Greek world. To the west is the Necropolis. Here the early hypogea of single families were soon turned into mass tombs, in order to accommodate the sheer numbers of Alexandrian dead. This tomb (above left), with 250 niches on two levels, is evidence of the unrelenting pressure on space.

motifs; there, a ceiling with friezes of cupids playing with dolphins, or a wall painted with a rustic scene of a child driving his oxen around the pivot of a *saqiya* or Persian wheel to raise water from the river. Greek traditions were observed, with an obol being placed on the deceased's tongue before burial, or cremation of the dead body. But over the centuries, as we have seen, the Greeks borrowed beliefs and customs from the Egyptians. The numerous mummies discovered in recent excavations are clear evidence of the change.

The faces of the dead stare out at us from plaster mummy cases, and from terracotta statuettes (the so-called 'Tanagra' figurines) of elegant Alexandrian ladies of the 3rd century BC. (Portraits painted in encaustic on wood, of the type known as 'Fayum

Some tombs with well preserved decoration show a mixture of Greek and Egyptian styles. Among the finest are those of Anfushi (left), built on the western tip of the island of Pharos in the 2nd century BC.

Dioscorides achieved the highest office under Ptolemy VI. Born of a Greek father and an Egyptian mother, he chose not to emphasize his Greek descent but instead to stress his Egyptian roots. His body was mummified and buried in the necropolis at Memphis in an anthropomorphic sarcophagus of black basalt, covered with hieroglyphic inscriptions recording the high points of his career.

portraits', were also produced in the capital, but because of the dampness of the soil they have not survived.) You can sense the families' affection, expressed in offerings such as oil lamps with which to brave the dark nether worlds, and incense burners. These are the same objects that are found in the houses of the living, and the tombs have the same painted walls, the same furniture, such as beds, and sometimes even the same rooms, like dining rooms where the living would gather to eat their meals in communion with the dead. The world of the dead is the mirror of the city of the living. Better preserved because it is underground, it shows us the Alexandrian way of life during the millennium of Greek and Roman rule.

Alexandrian trade and industry

Alexandria's prosperity depended on the exploitation of its fertile hinterland along the shores of Lake Mareotis, where wheat, vines and olive trees grew in abundance, satisfying the capital's immediate needs. Some of these goods were even exported, as we know from wine amphorae found as far away as the Gulf of Fos near Marseille. The popularity of Alexandrian wine is reflected in the poetry of Horace and Virgil, who sang the praises of the Mareotis vintage that they loved to drink at banquets in Rome.

In addition to this local trade across the lake, goods from all over the country were brought to Alexandria. The Ptolemies exploited Egypt as a whole – both the royal estates and land that was privately held, on which they imposed a variety of taxes. There were also royal monopolies, on oil for example. The country was run strictly, to the benefit of its ruler: all the products of the land, of which the most important was wheat, ended up in the warehouses of Alexandria, to be sold on elsewhere in the Mediterranean. Alexander's policy of opening up Egypt's Mediterranean coast had paid off.

The peace mission sent by Ptolemy I to the city of Nympheion in the Crimea involved enormous warships like the *Isis*, whose crew drew its picture there on the wall of a sanctuary of Apollo and Aphrodite – protectors of sailors – some time around 275–250 BC. Toward the rear of the ship (at the left) are four Macedonian shields and a soldier wearing a *petasus* and brandishing a lance. Faintly visible above is the Ptolemaic eagle, clutching Poseidon's trident in its claws.

On this partially gilt silver goblet, of the 1st century AD, satyrs and cupids gather bunches of grapes, carry the baskets to the vat, and tread the grapes, while the god Dionysus sits under a vine listening to musicians. Similar scenes took place in the estates and vineyards that lined the shores of Lake Mareotis.

Alexandrians also travelled to distant parts in search of rare commodities. Vast fleets – comprising more than 120 ships, according to Strabo – set sail from ports in the Red Sea for India, taking advantage of the monsoon winds on both legs of a voyage that lasted several months. They returned with exotic merchandise such as spices, precious stones, silks and ivory. A 3rd-century BC papyrus lists the composition of the cargo of a ship, the *Hermapollo*, newly returned from the port of Muziris on the western coast of India: it had on board 60 cases of the aromatic plant spikenard, 5 tons of other spices, more than 100 tons of elephants' tusks, and 135 tons of ebony.

This merchandise was destined for consumption in the capital, but also, more importantly, for the Mediterranean area. Alexandria was, in Strabo's phrase, the *emporium* or market of the world. There you could find goods from every part of the globe, especially luxury items with high added value. The products of local craftsmen further augmented the display of incomparable riches to be found for sale there.

Many ships were wrecked on the rocky shoals that surrounded the entrance to the port of Alexandria. From the contents of their cargoes – amphorae and urns of clay or bronze, fruit packed in sacks – it is possible to reconstruct the nature of the trade that took place between Alexandria and the Mediterranean world over a period of a thousand years, from the 4th century BC to the 7th century AD. Of great documentary value too is the customs list of the cargo of the *Hermapollo*, on its return from India in the 3rd century BC (above).

The Pharos, symbol of Alexandria's economic power

The Pharos or lighthouse of Alexandria was planned from the outset or very soon after the foundation of the city. It was a utilitarian structure, a stern necessity on this low-lying coast that lacked any landmark for approaching mariners, who had to make their way through reefs hidden just below the surface of the water. But at the same time it was a propaganda tool, its imposing height of 135 m (440 feet) demonstrating the power and strength of the new Greek authority

On coins, the Pharos is sometimes shown with two windowed storeys, sometimes with three. Invariably present, however, are the tritons on the lower balcony and the crowning statue.

This reconstruction of the Pharos is based on the latest research, according to which it comprised three sections (rectangular, octagonal and cylindrical) with access provided by a long ramp. Built between 297 and 283 BC, the tower was topped by a statue of Zeus. It was at once ranked among the seven wonders of the world, and was to survive for seventeen centuries, despite earthquakes, before finally collapsing in the first half of the 14th century.

that ruled over Egypt. Its construction was begun by Ptolemy I in 297 BC, and it was inaugurated fourteen years later, shortly after the death of the old king, by his son, Ptolemy II.

The ancient authors supply very little information about the Pharos, and Strabo's text is altogether too vague for the historian's purposes: he does however say that the Pharos was built of white stone, presumably the local limestone. Several authorities tell us there was a hearth on the top of the tower. But, as someone once said, the closer we get to this fire and to the light it shed, the more we moderns are plunged into the darkness of contradictory hypotheses and errors. How was the fire fuelled in a land with so few trees? Perhaps with naphtha, a form of petroleum that occurs naturally on the surface of ponds, which Herodotus in the 5th century BC tells us was used for heating and lighting? But even if we can imagine columns of draught animals bringing up the fuel, where would the hearth have been to which they were bringing it? Under the cupola or roof that supported the crowning statue? But in that case, how would it have been possible for the heat not to crack the stonework? And how could the flames resist the violent winds that afflicted Alexandria, not to mention the winter rains? All these questions remain unanswered, and only the discovery of new evidence, whether in the form of texts or archaeological remains, will make it possible to move beyond our current state of uncertainty as to the precise appearance of the Pharos.

This unique 1st-century AD glass goblet depicting the Pharos, with the statue on top, was presumably a souvenir of a visit to Alexandria, brought home by a Greek living in Afghanistan. It was formerly on show in the Kabul Museum, but has disappeared without trace, perhaps destroyed during the years of civil war, or more recently by the Taliban.

All the world's knowledge: the Library of Alexandria

It was the Ptolemies' desire to understand Egyptian civilization and that of its neighbours that led them to collect documents in different languages and bring together the world's finest scholars. They did this in order to govern more effectively, and hence more profitably. Their political ambition made Alexandria the intellectual and cultural capital of the world.

Under the guidance initially of the Athenian Demetrius of Phalerum, Ptolemy I conceived of a place that would bring together all the learning of the world under one roof. The scheme was carried on and expanded by his son Ptolemy II and their successors, up to the famous Cleopatra VII (69–30 BC). To add to his Library, Ptolemy II even required travellers arriving in Egypt to declare any manuscripts in their possession: any texts not already in the collection would then be copied before the manuscripts were returned to their owners – in theory at least, for it seems that not infrequently what the owner received was the copy.

Ptolemy III was desperate to get his hands on prime versions of the Greek classics, such as the great tragedies of Aeschylus, Sophocles and Euripides, and asked to borrow the manuscripts that were preserved with great care in one of the libraries of Athens.

No contemporary image exists of the Library and Mouseion in antiquity. But the theme inspired history painters such as Jean-Baptiste Champaigne, who in this painting (below left), shown at the Paris Salon of 1673, imagined a conversation between Ptolemy II and Jewish scholars about the Septuagint.

From the reign of Ptolemy I onwards, large numbers of Jews were attracted to Alexandria. They became thoroughly Hellenized and spoke only Greek, so Ptolemy II gave seventy rabbis the task of translating the Pentateuch, the five books of the Old Testament that made up the Torah. He is said to have shut the scholars away on the island of Pharos in seventy cells (right), whence they emerged with seventy translations identical in every respect. This apocryphal tale reflects the king's desire to collect translations for the Library of Alexandria. The Septuagint, the first Greek version of the Hebrew Bible, was in fact completed around 130 BC.

The Athenians, well aware of Ptolemy's collecting mania, demanded a deposit of 15 silver talents, a huge sum at that time. As soon as the manuscripts had safely reached Alexandria, Ptolemy sent his thanks to the Athenians and told them they were welcome to the deposit: he would be keeping the manuscripts.

Rolls of papyrus were collected in every tongue – Greek, Hebrew, Aramaic, Nabatean, Arabic, Indian languages, and, of course, Egyptian, reflecting the ethnic mix in the capital. From the outset, translations into Greek were commissioned. The most famous are those of the Jewish scriptures (the translation of the Old Testament is known as the Septuagint, because seventy scholars are supposed to have produced seventy versions of it, all absolutely identical), and those of the fragments that have come down to us of the genealogies

An inscription (left), found in Athens during excavations undertaken by the American School of Archaeology, proclaims that 'it is forbidden to take works out of the library', and also lists the opening times, from the 1st to the 6th hour. In Alexandria the Library was not open to the public, and the rules were equally strict. Not only could you not borrow books, but you might actually have a work you had brought with you confiscated and added to the collection.

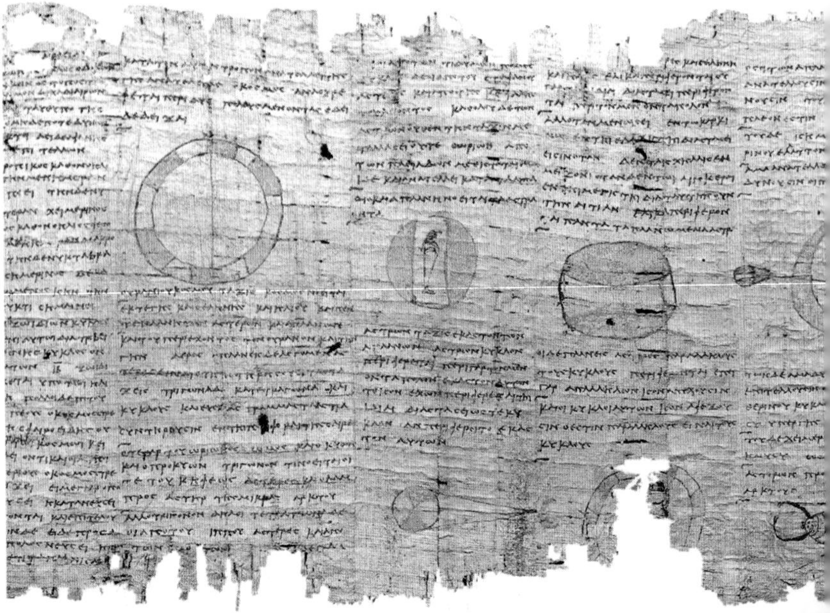

of the pharaohs, translated from the Egyptian by the priest Manetho.

Knowledge means power. That simple precept underlay the Ptolemies' desire to bring together the learning of the world under their exclusive control, something guaranteed to exacerbate their rivalry with other Hellenic cities. In Pergamon, the Attalid dynasty wanted to built up a library of their own, and to quash that ambition, the Ptolemies forbade the export of papyrus. The move was in vain, since the effect was to encourage their rivals to invent a new writing surface, which became known from the city's name as *pergamenon* – parchment.

This thirst for knowledge was not limited to the written word: it was also expressed in the resumption of the project to classify the world's flora and fauna that had been initiated by Aristotle and Theophrastus in Athens in the 4th century BC. The Ptolemies set up zoological gardens, and displayed particularly rare species during processions, as on the occasion of the

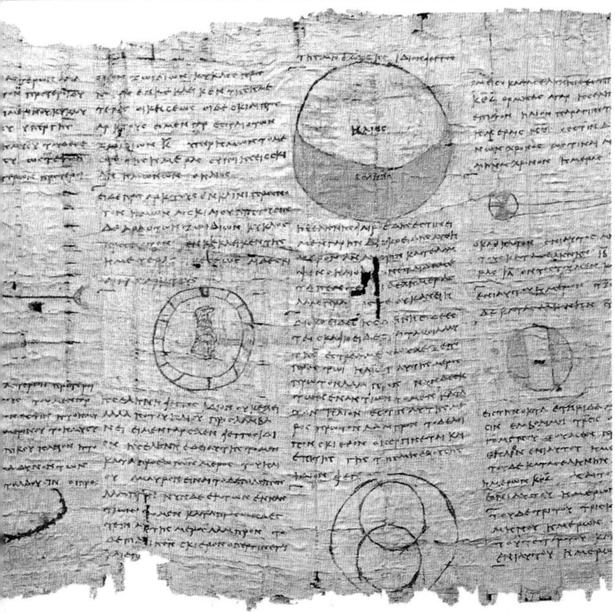

This 2nd-century BC papyrus (left), found in the Sarapeum in Memphis, is a copy of a treatise on astronomy by Eudoxus of Cnidos, a Greek scholar who had studied under the priests of Heliopolis during the reign of Nectanebo II, shortly before Alexander's conquest in 332 BC.

Ptolemaia of 270 BC, the funeral games held in honour of his father by Ptolemy II. He also created botanical gardens, where efforts were made to acclimatize plant species imported from other parts of the world, with the intention of growing them commercially, as we know from 3rd-century BC papyri.

The Library was not open to the public: instead, it was reserved for scholars invited from all over the world by the Ptolemies. They were based in the Mouseion, the research institute next to the Library, where they dedicated themselves to establishing authentic texts of Greek authors, for example removing from versions of Homer the annotations and commentaries that had crept in over the centuries. As well as philology, research was also undertaken in the mathematical sciences and astronomy.

A newly published papyrus (opposite below and below) contains a map of the Pyrenees with a description by the late 2nd-century BC geographer Artemidorus of Ephesus, as well as sketches of animals and a number of portraits. The drawings, in line, are of remarkable quality, reminiscent both of Renaissance works and of Macedonian tomb paintings. When items of this quality suddenly come to light, you realize just how many masterpieces must have been destroyed in the fire at the Great Library.

This painting from the Necropolis dates from the late 1st or early 2nd century AD. It shows a rural scene, with a *saqiya* being turned by a pair of oxen, urged on by a small boy. The wheel was used to raise water to irrigate the fields. The same system was employed at ground level above the cisterns of Alexandria. It is described in the *Hydraulica* of Heron of Alexandria. Much later, around 1800 AD, the scholars on Napoleon's expedition to Egypt observed similar *saqiya* in action, turned by dromedaries.

The first head of the Library, Eratosthenes, measured the difference in length of the shadow cast by his staff at the same time of day in Cyrene (the modern Aswan) and in Alexandria. Knowing the distance between the two points, he was able to deduce the arc and hence the circumference of the earth, plus or minus 2 per cent. Also in the 3rd century BC, Aristarchus of Samos calculated the distance between the earth and the moon, and realized they existed within a heliocentric system. In medicine, Herophilus performed dissections *in vivo* on men condemned to death, and deduced that the brain was the seat of intelligence and not the heart; he also isolated not only the nervous system but the arterial system.

The Mouseion attracted such famous names as Euclid and Archimedes of Syracuse, who as well as establishing the laws of geometry and physics were not too proud to investigate their applications, coming up with some wonderful devices such as the screw for raising water that is still used to irrigate the fields of the Nile Delta. One of the principal heirs of these engineers was Heron of Alexandria, who in the 1st century AD published works as various as the *Pneumatica*, in which he explains how to boil water and channel steam into a pipe, using this power to open the gates of a temple; the *Dioptra*, in which he describes the principles of magnifying lenses; the *Hydraulica*, in which he demonstrates the mechanism of a hydraulic lifting device; and the *Mechanica*, in which he specifies the number and size of pulleys necessary to lift a block of so many tons to a given height. The multifarious inventions he describes also include the famous magnets used to bring to life the statue of Sarapis in the Sarapeum.

The Mouseion was a crucible where the humanist ideas of Hellenic civilization interacted with the ancient civilization of Egypt (its mathematical and astronomical knowledge jealously preserved over the millennia by the priesthood), which the Greeks held in enormous regard – and to which their translations facilitated access. Alexandria and its Mouseion were responsible for a whole series of discoveries, sometimes forgotten in the centuries following the city's decline.

The date of the Library's destruction has long been a matter of debate. Caesar (100–44 BC) has been a suspect, because in his *De bello alexandrino* he describes how his troops set fire to a warehouse filled with papyrus scrolls near the port; but in fact the place he describes is clearly too far away to have been the Library. Another suspect is the Muslim general Amr ibn al-As, who conquered Alexandria in AD 642; but the stories about him are related by a Christian writer and cannot be trusted. Strabo was in Alexandria in 25 BC, and although he refers only to the Mouseion, it is likely that much of the information he supplies about Egypt comes from his researches in the Library; equally, if it had already been destroyed, he would surely have mentioned the fact. Once again we should probably think in terms of the violence and destruction that accompanied the wars between

Of the works of Heron of Alexandria, some hundred early copies

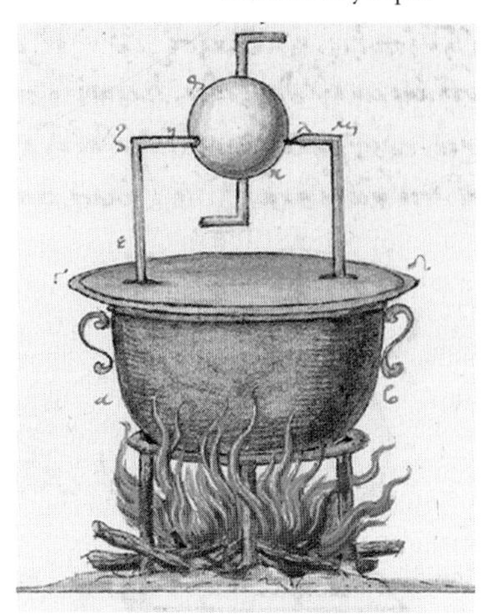

survive in European libraries. A 16th-century Greek manuscript includes this drawing demonstrating the motive power of boiling water.

A model shows the possibility, described in Heron's *Pneumatica*, of using steam to open the gates of a temple. This was steam power, more than sixteen hundred years before the British engineer James Watt invented his famous engines.

Zenobia of Palmyra and the Emperor Aurelian in the second half of the 3rd century, or the disturbances at the end of the century during the reign of Diocletian.

Alexandrian art

As well as importing art of every description, Alexandria was a centre of creativity. Its products were much admired, as we know from ancient sources and as we can see for ourselves from the Alexandrian artefacts discovered by archaeologists throughout the Mediterranean. The Alexandrian mosaic-makers produced medallions or *emblemas* made up of tiny cubes of coloured stone, glass and earthenware, and exported their masterpieces far and wide. The Roman scholar Pliny the Elder (AD 23–79) mentions the export trade in these Alexandrian *emblemas*, but until a few years ago experts believed that the technique had already died out by his time, and that Pliny was merely copying older sources. Recently, however, during a rescue dig at a house dating from around

The Alexandrians adored drama, and the city had some four hundred theatres. The repertoire included the Greek classics but also new plays by writers such as Menander. This faience figurine of an actor in the New Comedy dates from the second half of the 3rd century BC.

This masterpiece of Alexandrian mosaic work, of the 2nd century BC, came from one of the royal palaces and was found in 1993 during the building of the new Bibliotheca Alexandrina. It is the work of a master, who imitated an oil painting through the subtle hues of the minute tesserae of *opus vermiculatum*. The scene probably illustrates a fable: a domesticated dog (note the collar), with a contrite expression, sits back on his haunches, while a bronze vessel, or *askos*, lies overturned on the ground beside him.

AD 150, a disc was found with a mosaic picture of a Medusa's head set in clay, proving that such items continued to be made in the Roman era.

Goods of every kind contributed to the fame and wealth of the Ptolemaic capital – textiles, silks, sculptures in ivory and bone, carved gemstones and coral, and much else. A distinct stylistic development can be made out, as fashions changed during the Greek era.

The Macedonians who accompanied Alexander brought with them their own traditions and their own sense of design. Recent rescue digs have revealed what is effectively a Macedonian Alexandria. Then, as their customs and beliefs evolved over the centuries, the Alexandrian Greeks little by little imbibed Egyptian influence in the arts too, leading to an explosion of what could truly be called Greco-Egyptian art, sparkling with originality, full of subtlety and even humour. We should imagine the palace walls covered in blue-green ceramic tiles, and Egyptianizing decorative schemes with sphinxes and columnar statues of Ptolemies represented as pharaohs, but carved with purely Greek modelling – fortuitous combinations, creative exchanges, in the melting pot that was Alexandria, a city of syntheses in the arts as well as in the sciences of two mighty civilizations.

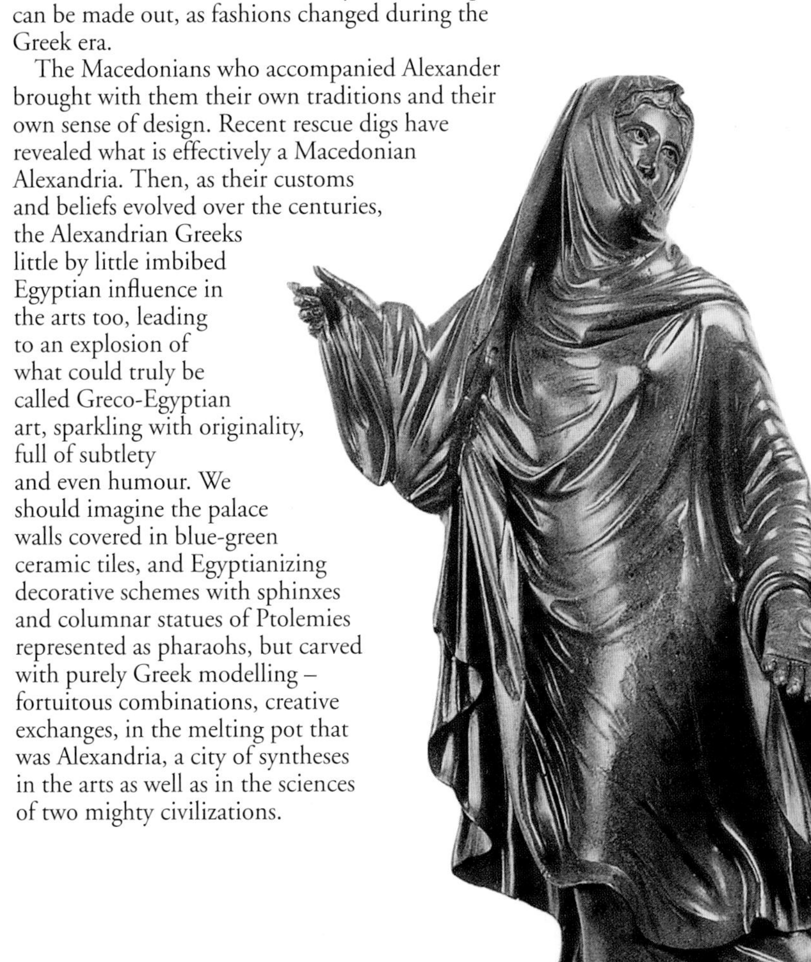

This bronze wall decoration shows an elegant lady wearing the *himation*, a cloak whose folds are cunningly arranged to show off the curves of her figure.

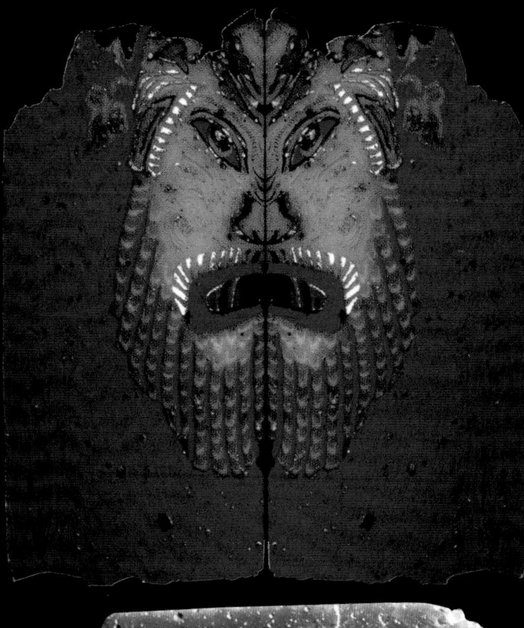

Ornamental glass work was an Alexandrian speciality. Reviving a pharaonic tradition, craftsmen manufactured flamboyantly decorated vessels and items in the variegated *millefiori* technique, and these appeared in the marketplaces of the Mediterranean world and beyond. Rods of glass in a variety of colours were clustered together and heated so that when they melted they produced images. The styles derived from both Greek and Egyptian iconography: here, for instance, we see heads of Dionysus (opposite), Silenus (left, above), and Horus the hawk. These tiny plaques of the 1st century BC, no more than 2.5 cm (1 inch) across, were inset in caskets and items of furniture, or used in murals.

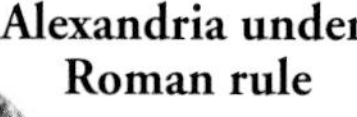

Alexandria under Roman rule

From 180 BC onwards Egypt experienced recurrent periods of unrest. These were sparked by economic crises that sowed discontent among the people, already reeling under the tax burden imposed by the Ptolemies; by a series of murders within the royal family that had the effect of weakening their power; and by intense pressure on the borders. The might of Rome was all that prevented the Seleucid Antiochus IV, ruler of neighbouring Syria, from besieging Alexandria. Increasingly it was the Romans who determined Egypt's destiny. Ptolemy XII, Cleopatra's father, kept his throne only because he had the support of wealthy Roman patrons, to whom he paid large sums of money.

Cleopatra VII's reign represented a last-ditch attempt to avoid a takeover over by Rome. In allying herself with Caesar her chief aim was to survive the determined attack of her two brothers. She clung to power first by conceiving Caesar's child, and then, after Caesar was assassinated in 44 BC, by capitalizing on the rivalry between the claimants to the throne, Octavian and Mark Antony. She won the latter's love (bearing him four children), but their joint ambitions led to a confrontation: the naval battle of Actium in 31 BC was the last time when the powers of East and West were balanced. Cleopatra saw her hopes founder, and

After his victory over Cleopatra and Mark Antony in the naval battle of Actium, Augustus had coins minted (left) with the inscription AEGYPT[O] CAPTA, arranged above and below a crocodile symbolizing Egypt. Statues of the victorious Octavian (below) were erected in the city, replacing those of Antony and Cleopatra, which were destroyed on his orders.

a year later Egypt's last queen followed Mark Antony to the grave, leaving the country in the hands of Octavian (who became Augustus three years later). Henceforward Egypt was to be the personal property of the emperor.

Alexandria ceased to be a capital, and was now merely the chief city of a province of the Roman Empire. Yet it remained an extraordinary place, acquiring ever more wealth through its far-flung trade with Africa and India. Merchandise from the rest of Egypt was stored here before being redistributed around the Mediterranean basin – Rome lived for four months of the year on grain from Alexandria. In the intellectual sphere, the Mouseion's reputation continued undimmed. The vitality of Alexandrian thought in all areas of knowledge continued undimmed: outstanding scholars in the 1st century AD were the engineer Heron (he of the many engines) and the Jewish philosopher Philo of Alexandria, and in the 2nd century the geographer Claudius Ptolemy. And when before long Christianity reached Alexandria, the city was to make a distinctive contribution to the development of Christian theology.

Like her predecessors, Cleopatra was represented sometimes in Greek guise and sometimes in the guise of a pharaoh, as in this relief at the temple of Dendara, of which she helped to finance the construction.

In the literary context within which Alexandrian Christianity evolved, Greek culture was the dominant influence. Like Philo of Alexandria before them, Clement and Origen were concerned to reconcile their faith with Platonic philosophy. The penetration of Alexandrian thought was to be crucial in determining the future of the emergent church and in defining its doctrines, even though on occasion it gave rise to heretical beliefs.

CHAPTER 2
CHRISTIAN ALEXANDRIA

On an ivory plaque of *c.* 600 (opposite), the Evangelist St Mark of Alexandria appears surrounded by thirty-five of his successors. In the background, the city's inhabitants look out from their windows and balconies.

Many offerings and inscriptions such as this cross in red paint (right) are to be found in the Necropolis, which had been the pagan cemetery, showing that it was taken over by Christians who used it in their turn to bury their own dead.

An early 2nd-century painting from a tomb in the catacombs of Kom es-Shoqafa, recorded in this copy, shows at the top a scene of mummification in pure pharaonic style, with the mummy laid out on a bed in the shape of a lion: Anubis carries out the procedure, with Isis and Nephthys beside him. In the lower register is a scene from Greek mythology. While Aphrodite remains impassive, her son Eros on her shoulder, Artemis brandishes her bow and Athena her lance, as they try to stop Hades, god of hell, from carrying off Persephone to his underworld kingdom.

Fertile ground

At the beginning of the Christian era, Alexandria was a cosmopolitan city, a melting pot in which all the peoples, languages and cultures of the ancient world coexisted. Its rich heritage was a blend of elements drawn from Greek philosophy, ancient Egyptian religion, the old religions of the East, and the new mystery cults.

A recent discovery in the catacombs of Kom es-Shoqafa sheds new light on the religious beliefs of Alexandrians at the start of the Roman era: paintings on a wall above two sarcophaguses depict, in two superimposed registers, a scene of the mummification of Osiris in pharaonic tradition, and a scene of the abduction of Persephone by Hades, both implying an eventual resurrection. These two cycles show the belief of an Alexandrian of the beginning of the 2nd century AD in an afterlife, conceived in both Egyptian and Greek versions. The ground was ripe for the Christian message, with its promise of the resurrection of the body on the Last Day.

The introduction of Christianity to Alexandria

According to tradition – which there is not enough documentation to confirm or refute – the Evangelist Mark taught in Alexandria before his martyrdom in *c.* AD 68. The first to become interested in Christianity were members of the Jewish community, who, until they were exterminated by Trajan in AD 116–117, formed a large and prosperous subsection of society. Indeed, so receptive were the Jews to the new religion that it was perceived as a branch of Judaism.

The speed with which the Christian message spread to Alexandria is partly explained by the fact that the Alexandrian Jews had maintained close links with their coreligionists in Palestine. But the new religion was not for the chosen people alone, and before long the pagans followed their example. First were the Greeks, who were close to the Hellenized Jews; then the Egyptians, a people whose intensely religious nature had been recognized by Greek writers from Herodotus onwards, were seduced by this Messiah who rose again from the dead, like their god Osiris.

A 'Church' was soon established (the earliest sources we have for this are from the 2nd century) under the authority of a bishop elected by the community, which also chose priests and deacons. This bishop represented the Alexandrian community, just as other bishops

St Mark preaching in Egypt is the subject of this 16th-century painting by the Venetian artists Gentile and Giovanni Bellini. The setting looks very Italian, despite the campaniles in the shape of minarets. In 968, Venetian merchants stole the remains of St Mark from the patriarchate of Alexandria. Tradition has it that they transported them in a barrel, passing easily through customs by claiming it was filled with pork. A basilica dedicated to the saint was built in Venice. In 1968 the Pope returned some of the remains to the Orthodox Coptic Patriarch.

headed the Churches of the principal cities of the Eastern Empire – Jerusalem, Antioch and Constantinople. None held primacy. They assembled, sometimes in the company of bishops from the Western Empire, first in synods, then in councils, where attempts were made to define a dogma that would apply to the entire Christian community.

The Didascalia emerged in *c.* 180 as a school for instruction in the beliefs of the new faith, rivalling the teachings of the scholars at the Mouseion and of the pagan professors. Under Clement in the 2nd century and Origen in the early 3rd century, it laid down certain fundamental principles in which Greek tradition was married to Christian precepts. The Didascalia was both the institution where the converted were instructed in the new faith and a school of philosophy which made Alexandria a celebrated centre of early Christian theology.

The persecution of the Christians

In the first three centuries of the Empire, the life of a Christian in Alexandria was anything but easy: the persecutions that began in AD 64 continued up to and even beyond Diocletian's campaign of repression, which was felt with particular severity in Alexandria.

The 3rd-century Christian paintings that decorated the catacombs of Kom es-Shoqafa, now destroyed, are known through copies made in the 1860s such as this one (below). On the left is the wedding at Cana; in the middle, the miracle of the loaves and fishes.

St Catherine is not recorded in history, but she became the object of a fervent cult, generating an extensive iconography. Frescoes by Masolino in San Clemente in Rome, of the 15th century, show her instructing the teachers of the Didascalia (opposite), and preparing for her martyrdom on the wheel (left).

The Emperor Diocletian (below) was responsible for an extensive reorganization of the Empire. He recaptured Alexandria from a usurper in 297, after a long siege. The Copts commemorated his cruel persecution of Christians by starting their calendar on the first day of his reign.

These bloody events are commemorated in the Coptic calendar: it starts in AD 284, that being the first year of Diocletian's reign and the beginning of the 'era of martyrs'. The persecutions were pursued by Diocletian's successors: in the years following his abdication in 305, Galerius and Maximian Daia were fanatical in their implementation of his policy, which continued unabated in Egypt until 313.

There were many martyrs, most of them obscure but some famous, like St Catherine of Alexandria. Bishops were put to death by the civil authority: Bishop Peter, regarded as the last in a long line of martyrs, was executed in 311. A *martyrium* was built in the Necropolis to hold his remains, and here the Christians sought asylum,

The monastery of St Menas, or Abu Mina (left, ruins of the 5th-century basilica), was a place of pilgrimage until the 10th century. Since Helena, mother of the Emperor Constantine, had been cured there of dropsy, people visited the saint in the expectation of a miracle. St Menas was a 3rd-century legionary who converted to Christianity. After martyrdom in Asia Minor, his body was returned to his family in Egypt, but the two camels transporting it suddenly refused to proceed (below), indicating that this was where the saint should be laid to rest. The monastery was later built on the site.

in the hypogea that dated back to the city's foundation. Hounded out of the city, they took over the pagan tombs and used them to bury their own dead.

Monasticism

One way of escaping persecution was to take refuge in the desert. Before long the practice was being embraced voluntarily, as the solitude and privation seemed to provide the ideal means of restraining the passions and promoting meditation and detachment from the contingent realities of everyday life. Thus Egyptian monasticism was born, soon institutionalized by the founding of monastic communities that set themselves to survive in this remote and hostile environment. In the early 4th century the monastery of St Menas was established, a large foundation some 50 km (30 miles) southeast of Alexandria, which attracted many pilgrims. Others chose to pursue a religious vocation by becoming hermits. St Anthony and St Paul are famous examples of voluntary recluses who lived alone for decades in the Egyptian desert.

The example of Egyptian monasticism was emulated in Palestine, Syria, Asia Minor (with the foundation by St Basil of a monastery at Caesarea in 357), in Constantinople itself, and even in North Africa (by St Augustine). With the visit to Rome of Athanasius, bishop of Alexandria, in 341, the principles of the monastic life became known to the West. It seems that during his exile he met Martin, the future bishop of Tours, and conceived the notion of founding the first monastery in the Western world at Ligugé (in 360), followed by a community on a larger scale at Marmoutier (372). The practice that originated in Egypt was subsequently to spread throughout the West.

Origen (here in a manuscript of *c.* 1100) was, after Clement of Alexandria, among the earliest heads of the Didascalia. This school of religious instruction before long came to rival the pagan Mouseion, and it attracted the attention of the Greek world to its teachers, who were steeped in Greek culture. However, it was not long before the ideas of the Alexandrian Church Fathers began to offend the hierarchy. Origen was banished to Caesarea by the patriarch Demetrius; his later writings were deemed to deviate from official doctrine.

The 4th century: the Church triumphant

The accession of the Emperor Constantine (?285–337) marked the beginning of a new era in the history of the Church. Persecutions became a thing of the past and, in 313, Constantine pronounced an edict allowing freedom of worship. Christianity became a central element of imperial policy. The emperor intervened in theological debates, and forced the bishops to agree on the nature of the Christian faith. Alexandria was to play a major role in the working out of Christian doctrine, not least because certain deviant interpretations originated in the Alexandrian Church. The official recognition granted to Christianity was thus accompanied by violent dissension, stemming not from external forces but from within the Christian camp itself.

In the 4th century, the emperors took part in decisions that affected the Church. This 9th-century manuscript shows Constantine presiding over the Council of Nicaea. He is seated on the imperial throne, and his crowned head is encircled with a halo. With him are the patriarchs of Constantinople, Antioch, Jerusalem and Alexandria. At the bottom, the heretical books of the Arians are being burned on Constantine's orders.

First crisis: the Arian heresy

Between 323 and 381, the Church was under grave threat from the Arian heresy. The Alexandrian presbyter Arius had advanced the belief that only God the Father was *agennetos*, 'not born' or 'not created', while the Son had a dual nature, being divine but also created by the Father. This doctrine became hugely popular, winning over many of the bishops. The Council of Nicaea, held in 325, condemned Arius and declared that the Son was *homoousios* – 'begotten, not made'. Athanasius, patriarch of Alexandria from 328, was to devote his life to the struggle against Arianism. With the Byzantine authorities adopting an ambivalent attitude towards divisions in the Alexandrian Church

Theophilus, Bishop of Alexandria, implemented the imperial decree to close pagan temples by sacking the most famous sanctuary in Alexandria, the temple of the city's god, Sarapis, which had been founded by Ptolemy 1 seven centuries earlier. An Egyptian manuscript, probably of the 8th century (opposite), shows him standing majestically on top of the sanctuary, in which the figure of the ancient bearded god is set between two columns under a triangular pediment.

(perhaps to weaken it and impose the authority of Constantinople), it all but carried the day. The violent controversy left deep scars, but the official Church in the end emerged victorious. The result, however, simply put off for a time the confrontation between the ecclesiastical hierarchy and the aspirations of the people.

Destruction of the pagan temples

In 391–392 the Emperor Theodosius banned pagan cults. In Alexandria, the results were quickly felt. Bishop Theophilus led his troops in an attack on the place that had been the great pagan symbol ever since the city's foundation seven centuries earlier: he ordered the sanctuary of Sarapis to be sacked, and on its ruins founded a monastery dedicated to St John. On the Caesareum, the sanctuary dedicated to the cult of the emperor, right in the heart of the city, he built a church.

After two centuries in which the Christians had been persecuted, now, in a complete reversal, Christianity was brutally imposed on the population and the pagans were put to flight; pagan philosophy, too, was under attack. There were bloody encounters. The martyrs now were the pagans, among them the famous woman philosopher Hypatia, who in 415 was torn to pieces by a horde of black-robed monks in the streets of Alexandria, on the orders of Theophilus' successor, Bishop Cyril.

The churches of Alexandria

The early Christians assembled in private houses or in the cemeteries, around the martyrs' graves. From the mid-3rd century on, and especially in the following century, the community began to build places of worship inside the city. Many Christian churches were built on the actual site of pagan temples, or in quarters of the city named after those temples. Little or no archaeological remains have been found to date, so we have to rely on written sources. From these we learn of a dozen or so churches, some built within an ancient pagan sanctuary, such as the Caesareum, or the temple of Kronos Saturn, which was made to house the church of St Michael (the archangel replacing the god Thoth); the Mendideion was built in or near the sanctuary of the oriental deity Bendis. Other religious buildings were named after the quarter where they were erected (e.g. Baukalis), or the donor (Sarapion, Anianos), or the bishop who founded them, such as Denys or Theonas, who built the first bishop's palace to the west of the city. The cemeteries continued to serve as meeting places, especially the two *martyria*, that of St Mark to the east and its symmetrical counterpart to the west, in the Necropolis, where the church of the martyred Bishop Peter of Alexandria was built among the hypogea.

The falcon-headed god Horus, on horseback, plunges his lance into a crocodile, the creature associated with the evil god Seth, on a 4th- or 5th-century relief – an Egyptian equivalent of the archangel Michael slaying the dragon.

The birth of the Coptic Church

The Council of Nicaea in 325 established that the bishop of Alexandria was the primate of Egypt, but it also declared the primacy within the Byzantine Church as a whole of the bishop of Constantinople. Subjection to that central authority became a source of conflict between the Egyptians and the Greeks.

The Council of Chalcedon in 451 provoked the secession of the Alexandrian Church. Up till then

the Egyptians had put up with the control exercised by the authorities in Constantinople, who had ruled the country since the Roman Empire was officially divided in 395. While civil control was imposed if necessary by force of arms, the Church functioned in a rather more democratic fashion. Since the 3rd century translations of the Christian texts into the vernacular had been available (for this a new script was used, adapted from the Greek), and certain positions were filled by election. It was not long before the Egyptians formed a majority, and were able to take over the running of the institution.

The city of Alexandria is depicted in schematic form on a mosaic of 531 AD found at Gerash in Jordan. Houses and domed buildings, the city's first churches, are jumbled together inside the walls, which are fortified with towers.

Until the 5th century, the officials of the Egyptian Church were all Greek. Difficulties set in in 444 when an Egyptian called Dioscorus was elected as patriarch: the situation was intolerable to the Greeks, and they took immediate action. The Byzantine authorities could not be indifferent to the emergence of what looked to them suspiciously like a national Church,

A capital (opposite) of Marmara marble, thought to have come from St Mark's Church in Alexandria, is a typical example of 4th-century Constantinopolitan art.

which might eventually challenge the authority of Constantinople.

The conflict crystallized around an issue of dogma. The Egyptians under Dioscorus refused to recognize the dual nature, both human and divine, of the single person of Christ. They were called Monophysites, and were declared heretics by the emperors in Constantinople. Dioscorus was deposed and exiled.

A mural of Christ in Majesty from the monastery of St Jerome at Saqqara shows his index finger touching his thumb, symbolizing his dual nature, human and divine.

In his place the Greeks installed a Hellene, Proterios. The Egyptians held back until the death of Proterios in 457, but then proceeded to elect their own patriarch, Timotheus II, thereby challenging the authority of the patriarch appointed by the Greeks. Ever since there have been two lines of patriarchs, Coptic and Greek Orthodox (the latter known as Melchite, or 'royal', after the Arab conquest of 641), both of whom claimed to be the heirs of St Mark.

Until the Arab conquest, the Alexandrian Church continued to be controlled by Greeks. The same applied to its dependencies nearby, such as the monastery of St Menas, to the larger towns of the province, and to a few isolated pockets such as the monastery of St Catherine on the Sinai peninsula. Greeks tended to cling on to power where there was a high level of Hellenization within the community. The rest of the country, however, was firmly in the hands of the Copts, and Alexandria itself was retaken in the confusion surrounding the Arab invasions. The consequences for the Greek community that had lived in and governed the city for a thousand years were dire. Their day was over: the Coptic patriarch was in a position of power, and indeed the Melchite patriarchate disappeared altogether between 642 and 727. After that, the Greeks had restricted access to places of worship taken over by the national Church. The new masters of the country, the Arabs, clearly understood the situation: it was they who invented the word 'Copt', from the Greek *Aigyptoi* ('Egyptians') – designating the community not by their religion but by their nationality.

A bewildering range of religious beliefs and cults was imported into Alexandria by the city's cosmopolitan population. Devotees of Ahura Mazda, Manichaeans, worshippers of Mithras, all rubbed shoulders with members of the various Christian sects. Among the latter was Gnosticism, whose importance is confirmed by the codices of Nag Hammadi (below). This doctrine, strongly opposed by Clement of Alexandria, posited the opposition between the evil world created by the god of the Old Testament and a perfect world, the *pleroma*, from which humankind was cut off by the fall of an *eon*, an emanation of the divine, associated with 'Wisdom' or *Sophia*.

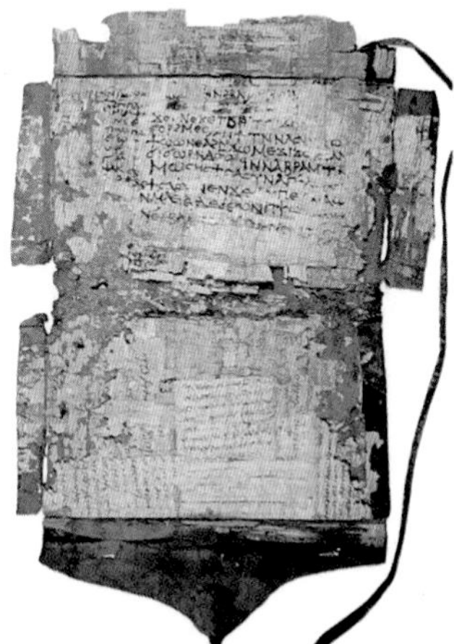

‘Alexandria is a jewel of manifest brilliance, and a virgin decked with glittering ornaments. She lights up the West with her glory; she combines beauties of the most diverse description, because of her situation between Orient and Occident. There every wonder is displayed for all eyes to see, and there all rare things arrive.’

Ibn Battuta, *Travels in Asia and Africa* (1325–54)

CHAPTER 3
ARAB AND OTTOMAN ALEXANDRIA

Alexandria and its Pharos appear in a Turkish manuscript of 1582 (opposite). In the late 12th century, Saladin established foundations for pilgrims and merchants from the Maghreb who had come to settle in Alexandria (right, the dedication on a foundation stone); in 1183 Ibn Jubayr praised the city's schools and monasteries, founded by benefactors from 'the most far-flung lands'.

The Arab armies began their conquest of Egypt in 639 without meeting any great resistance, but Alexandria's city walls presented a more substantial obstacle to general Amr ibn al-As, and it took him several months before he finally conquered the capital in the autumn of 641. In much the same way as Egypt had submitted to Alexander the Great in 332 BC, to rid itself of the Persian yoke, now it hoped its conquerors would deliver it from Greco-Roman rule. The country's new masters, nomads from the Arabian peninsula, were baffled by this megalopolis: it was a new world that inspired both admiration and suspicion. Sultan Uthman indeed forbade Amr from keeping his troops too long inside its walls, and as a result the Byzantine general Manuel recaptured it in 645. He was dislodged only after another long period of siege, Amr having been called back to the rescue.

Alexandria, known as 'Iskanderiyya' in Arabic, became a provincial Egyptian town, subordinate to the new capital, Fustat, on the site of modern Cairo.

Administration

Alexandria did remain a *polis*: it enjoyed city status, with a governor assisted by a civil and religious judge, or *qadi*, a harbour captain and an official in charge of customs. In the years following the conquest, the Arabs kept in place as prefect (*muqawqis*) the Byzantine patriarch Cyrus, and after him another Greek who bore the title *augustalios*. When the Umayyad dynasty

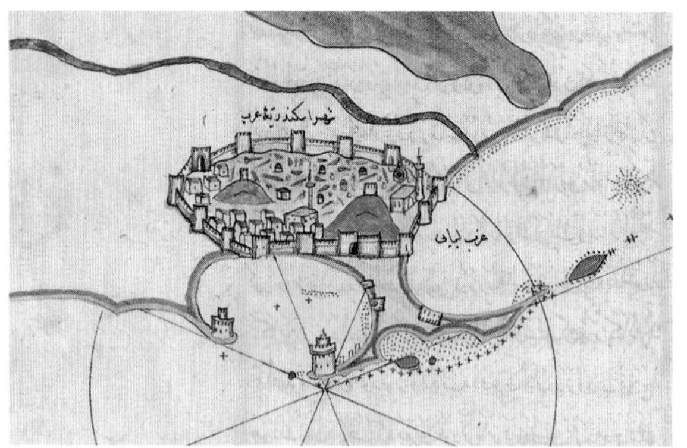

In the 9th century new city walls were built, encompassing a much smaller area than the earlier fortifications; this Turkish map shows the city from the north. Recent excavations have found trenches where old stones were dug out for re-use in this major work of construction, whose fame spread far and wide. The new Alexandria was to enjoy more than five hundred years of prosperity, functioning as the outer harbour first of Fustat and then of Cairo, until the arrival of the Ottomans in 1517.

The Fatimids – seen here in a confrontation with crusaders – ruled from Cairo for two hundred years. In the 12th century they were succeeded by the Ayyubids, of whom the most illustrious was Saladin, who pushed back the crusaders, recaptured Jerusalem, and strengthened Alexandria's perimeter walls to prevent incursions.

In 1365, Peter I of Lusignan, king of Cyprus, launched a raid on Alexandria aimed at disrupting his rival's trading routes. Pillaging went on for two days, until the arrival of Mamluk reinforcements from Cairo.

came to power, the post was occupied by a Muslim, or less frequently by a Copt. Under Ibn Tulun the city achieved a high level of autonomy, which it retained until the 10th century, but it lost this relative independence when the Fatimids fell in 1171. Alexandria then became a *taghr*, or frontier town, a fortress for the pursuit of holy war against the Franks.

Alexandria offered a very tempting target, attracting forays, raids and attempts at invasions (the Normans from Sicily in 1153 and 1155, then the Pisans, and the Normans again in 1174), inspired either by the desire for plunder or with the aim of disrupting the trade routes that passed through Alexandria.

The urban fabric

The chroniclers and travellers of the 9th to the 13th centuries left no more than general descriptions. It is possible to deduce from the odd phrase that the Arabs were dazzled at the sight of the city, whose construction and monuments must have seemed to them the work of a supernatural power, but that this did not stop them from making practical use of the magnificent remains: in the 8th century, we know that a bronze statue was melted down to make coins, when metal was in short supply.

Engraved views of Alexandria, copying one another, were produced from the 16th century onward. They show the canal entering the city from the north and spreading out into five branches inside the walls with their many battlements and towers. In the middle is a complex of mosques and some scattered houses; out at sea, Arab and European ships. To the right, in the background outside the walls, stands Pompey's Pillar.

The ancient royal palaces were abandoned, and the new seat of government was situated at the opposite end of the city, to the west: grouped together there were the palace or Dar al-Sultan, the arsenal, the dockyard, and the customs house. Arab policy in Alexandria focused exclusively on frontier defence, tax collection, and the levying of customs duties. A minimum of maintenance of the urban fabric could nevertheless not be avoided – repairs to the walls, the Pharos, the ports and the canal.

Ibn Tulun, or his father, was responsible for new city walls which reduced the urban area by half. These walls, equipped with a hundred or so towers, were maintained and extended over the centuries, by Saladin (1171–93), Baybars (1260–76), Sha'ban (1363–76), and, not long before the Ottoman invasion, Qaitbay (1468–96) and al-Ghuri (1501–16).

Alexandria's walls made a great impression on travellers. Bernhard von Breydenbach, dean of the cathedral of Mainz, who saw them on his way to the Holy Land in 1483, wrote: 'Once inside the town, we were amazed to see all about us nothing but miserable ruins; we could not contain our astonishment at seeing such fine and strong walls surrounding such a poor town' (*Pilgrimage to the Holy Land*, 1486).

Churches were taken over and turned into mosques: the great mosque to the east, al-Djami el-Gharbi, was formerly the church of Theonas, while the Attarine Mosque occupied the site of the church of St Athanasius. One of the first acts of General Amr had been to build a mosque; this was pulled down by Sultan al-Hakim in 1004 and replaced by a grander building. Some of the sultans were patrons of architecture, following the example of Saladin, who built a hospital, school and guesthouse to accommodate the influx of people from the Maghreb (North Africa).

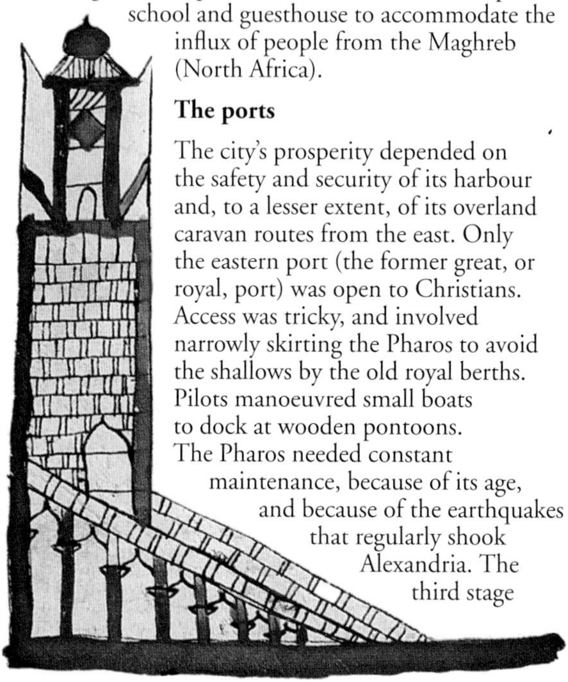

The ports

The city's prosperity depended on the safety and security of its harbour and, to a lesser extent, of its overland caravan routes from the east. Only the eastern port (the former great, or royal, port) was open to Christians. Access was tricky, and involved narrowly skirting the Pharos to avoid the shallows by the old royal berths. Pilots manoeuvred small boats to dock at wooden pontoons. The Pharos needed constant maintenance, because of its age, and because of the earthquakes that regularly shook Alexandria. The third stage collapsed and was transformed by Ibn Tulun into a mosque. Saladin reconstructed it in part, as did Baybars, who when the second stage was destroyed built a mosque directly on the terrace of the first level. The violent quake of 1303 inflicted a fatal blow. Ibn Battuta, from Tangier, tells us that in 1329 he could get up to the door on the first floor, but that this was impossible when he returned to Alexandria in 1346.

In the late 9th century, Yakubi of Baghdad described the admiration he felt at the sight of the Pharos: 'Among these prodigious buildings is the Pharos, which stands by the sea at the entrance to the great port. It is a strong, well-built tower, 175 cubits in height, at the top of which is a hearth in which fires are lit when the watch sights ships far out to sea.' Ibn Jubayr climbed to the mosque at the top of the tower on 1 April 1185: the oratory, he says, is 'famous for bringing good luck, which people seek by performing ritual prayers'. At the same period, another traveller, known as al-Andalusi – 'the Andalusian' – visited Alexandria and gave the most detailed description we have of the Pharos. A 16th-century manuscript of his text is enriched with vignettes that depict the building: this one shows the ramp leading up to the entrance door, and the three levels topped by a cupola.

After the Pharos collapsed, shipping movements were kept under surveillance from a manmade hill called Kom el-Nadura, literally 'hill of the watch'. On the eastern side of the harbour, the Mamluk sultan Qalaun in 1365 built another fort, which travellers christened the 'Pharillon' or little Pharos.

The western port, the ancient *Eunostos*, was reserved for Muslim craft. The obsession with security was so great that an iron chain barred its entry: on the southern edge of the lagoon lay the shipyard and the warships that had to be kept safe at all costs from Frankish raids.

Population

The historian Ibn Abd al-Hakam, writing in the 9th century, put the number of Greeks at the time of the Arab conquest at 600,000, and Jews at 40,000. These figures need to be viewed with caution, however: in the 12th century the Jew Benjamin of Toledo speaks of just 3,000 Jews; 13th-century sources indicate 60,000 inhabitants in all, although the population had just been reduced by plague; in the 14th century, the total is again given as 50,000–60,000 inhabitants.

The figures fluctuate, but they fall a long way short of the estimated population of ancient Alexandria, reflecting a process of depopulation that was to accelerate in the following centuries.

At the time of the Arab conquest, there is no doubt that the Copts formed the majority.

In the medieval period, Alexandria was a focus of maritime trade. An Arabic manuscript of 1237 shows a merchant ship with an Indian crew and Arab passengers in the Persian Gulf.

'When you enter Alexandria, you see a handsome fort [below] with twenty-two towers and a wall ten cubits thick between the towers . . . I have never seen such a handsome fortress, just three years old; eight hundred Mamluks sleep there every night.'

Anonymous traveller, 15th century

•These *funduks* [left] are rather square in shape and bear a strong resemblance to *khans*, but inside they are planned differently, with walkways and different floors, two or three, one above the other, with rooms all around in which the merchants are accommodated; on the lower levels are simple vaults, each independent of the rest, in which each merchant shuts up his wares. These places are called stores. In the middle is a place where the merchants put out, exchange, wrap and unwrap their wares. Every evening when it grows dark, the servants of the emir and the lord of the city come and shut up all the *funduks*, so the merchants will not be ill-treated by the pagans.•

Joos van Ghistele from Flanders, *c.* 1480

They managed to reach an accommodation with their new masters, and succeeded in keeping their own religion. (The large numbers of conversions in the 8th and 13th centuries were in part a manœuvre to escape the poll tax.) They remained active in commerce and even held official positions.

People from the Maghreb and Andalusia encountered Alexandria on the pilgrimage route to Mecca, and came to settle there in large numbers, setting up trade links with their native countries. This was encouraged by the authorities, in particular the Fatimids, from Morocco, who captured Egypt in 969 and ruled it for two centuries. Succeeding sultans too treated them with consideration, following the example of Saladin, who provided shelter for their community, because their trading activities brought substantial revenues to the government in power.

The Bedouin occupied the suburbs and the desert areas on

the edge of the Delta. They controlled trade on the overland route and, in the event of trouble, would be called on to sort out – often brutally – any problems experienced by the authorities. They were rarely to be seen in the city, but their presence made itself felt whenever Alexandria needed to have dealings with the rest of the country.

Finally, there were the so-called 'Franks', or Christians from Western Europe. They were few in number, no more than a couple of hundred, yet they occupied a large area. They were merchants – Venetians, Frenchmen, Catalans, Pisans, and others. In the 13th century, there were representatives from twenty eight different 'Frankish' towns in Alexandria. The Frankish communities came under the authority of their consuls, and they lived in *khans* or *funduks* reserved for their use. They could not go out on the streets after dusk, but they had their own churches and were protected by the authorities; if their fate remained sometimes precarious, because of attacks by patrolling fleets or by pirates, in general their rights and safety were assured by the authorities: they were well treated because they too paid a lot in taxes.

In 1183, Ibn Jubayr tells us, Alexandria possessed twelve thousand mosques according to some, eight thousand according to others; 'they are indeed very numerous, four or five on the same spot, and sometimes one comprises several'. Two mosques there in his time were the Attarine Mosque (opposite, below), on the site of the church of St Athanasius, and the mosque of Abu Ali (below).

The Muslim religion

The new rulers brought with them a new religion. The three religions of the Book were now all officially recognized – Islam, Judaism and Christianity. The conquerors, who came from Arabia, were Sunnis, but by the 8th century the influence of Shiites from the Maghreb was making itself felt. Under the Fatimids, concerned with *jihad* (holy war launched on behalf of a city under threat from the crusades), this became the dominant strand. A new movement grew up in Alexandria known as the *Shadiliyya*, which was introduced by a Moroccan and developed by his successor, the Andalusian Abu el-Abbas el-Morsi; the latter, who died in Alexandria in 1287 and is buried in the largest mosque, is still

The Lithuanian Jew Samuel Jemsel visited Alexandria in 1641 and noted that 'the Mohammedans there have thirty mosques, among which there is one that is supported on a thousand marble columns'.

regarded as the patron saint of the city. With the arrival of the Mamluks in the mid-13th century, however, the focus of power shifted back to Cairo, and the Alexandrian school moved to the capital.

In parallel, after a brief spell in the Delta, the Coptic patriarchate too was transferred to Cairo in the 8th century. This was not an authoritarian or penal measure, but simply a reflection of the new political and economic reality: money and power were concentrated in the new capital.

Greek Christians – the Melchites or 'royalists' who formerly controlled the country – had ceased to exist. After the Arab conquest and the death of Cyrus,

Below: weighing goods in Fatimid Egypt.

Opposite: the weaving of *tiraz* (bands of cloth used to decorate formal robes) was a state monopoly. These luxury fabrics were exported all over the world. In the Middle Ages, one of the vestments of the popes in Rome incorporated Alexandrian silk brocade.

Orthodox patriarch and prefect of Alexandria, the Greek patriarchate disappeared entirely for nearly a century.

A time of great prosperity

Recent archaeological finds have altered our perception of the history of medieval Alexandria. While it certainly lost its position as Egypt's first city, excavations reveal an abundance of merchandise imported from all over the world, from *Ifriqiyya* (Morocco) in the west to China in the east (celadon ware has been found), a trade that continued on a large scale until the end of the 14th century.

Tolls provided the sultans with a major source of income. From the 11th century onwards, Pisa, Genoa and Venice all traded directly with Alexandria for their food supplies. In the 14th century, al-Makrisi states that a single Frankish ship could bring in up to 40,000 dinars in duties. This was no doubt an exceptional case, but it is estimated that, year in, year out, the sultans could count on more than 100,000 dinars in import and export duties.

The production of silks, much-prized brocades, cotton and wool textiles was an important local industry; in the 15th century there were as many as 14,000 looms, but the competition of cheaper woollen cloth from Flanders and England was to make itself acutely felt in the following century. Alum was another export, as were natron (used in cloth production), spices (especially pepper, of which the Venetians bought more than 1,500,000 pounds in a single year), herbs, coral (which was particularly popular in the Far Eastern market), pearls, mercury, and slaves.

Alexandria's Jewish merchants were very active as middlemen. Archives surviving from the 12th and 13th centuries reveal a constant exchange of people and of information between the capital and Alexandria, even though the journey took a week to complete (express couriers could make the return journey in a week).

❛Alexandria is the main port of the kingdom of Egypt. Many sorts of merchandise are brought there, in particular pepper and other spices that come from Cairo by the Nile. Here both the friends of the Turks and their enemies too can trade, because it is a "free port." Ragusan, Sicilian and Neapolitan vessels, ships from Livorno, Genoa and other Christian cities on the sea come here, along with French, Venetian and English craft. All have freedom to move about openly, on condition that they present and contribute to their respective consuls the percentage due to them; [in return] the latter give them protection and safe conduct.❜

Johann Wild,
a German from
Nuremberg,
enslaved in Egypt
1606–10

The determination of the central government to protect the agents of commerce is no doubt the explanation for the city's prosperity in the medieval period. In the Arab world, however, the major centres of economic activity were not coastal cities. By now Alexandria was in effect no more than the outer port for Cairo, sending goods on to the secure warehouses of distant Fustat. But this city on the Mediterranean, with its large sheltered ports, continued to exploit those natural advantages that had attracted settlers to it in the ancient world.

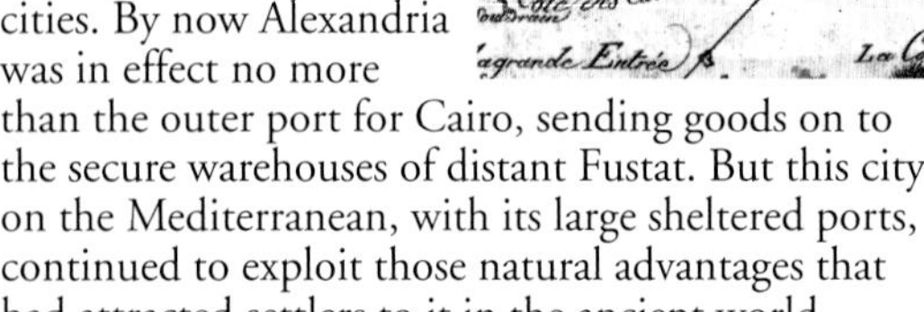

On this 18th-century navigational map, produced in Marseille, the 9th-century walls are still visible, but the city itself is now confined to the isthmus occupied by the Ottomans in 1517.

Ottoman Alexandria

The Mamluks, in power since 1251, came under threat from the Ottoman Turks. Expecting an attack from the sea, Sultan Ashraf Qaitbay constructed a chain of little forts along the coast, among them one at Rosetta. In 1477 he built a castle on the foundations of the Pharos. When the Turks eventually came, however,

The mosque of Abd el-Latif (17th–18th century) was recorded in 1822 by the French architect/engineer Pascal Coste. Typically, the mosques of Alexandria show strong influence from the architecture of the Maghreb region, which is not surprising, since they were often endowed by wealthy merchants from the Maghreb who had settled in the city. They are built of brick, red or black according to the method of firing, and set on an upper storey, with shops at ground level (as in the Shorbagi Mosque), and their interiors are faced with Tunisian and Moroccan tiles.

they arrived overland. Selim I crossed the Sinai and seized Cairo, before sending his emissaries to secure Alexandria in 1517.

The shape of the city changed. The Turks did not move into the areas inside the 9th-century walls, among the ruins of the Greco-Roman houses. Instead, they preferred to build on the spit of land that had been formed by silting-up on either side of the Heptastadion, the ancient causeway linking the city to the island of Pharos. On this virgin ground, they used materials taken from the ancient city to build what the scholars who accompanied Bonaparte's expedition in 1798–1801 dubbed the 'new city'. Gradually, as successive maps show, virtually the entire population shifted to this area.

Alexandria ceased to have a hinterland; as soon as you left the city walls behind, you ran the risk of being set upon by a horde of Bedouin. By *c.* 1650 the canal that linked the city to the Nile ceased to be navigable, through lack of maintenance. The pashas appointed by Istanbul did not stay in place long enough to undertake major works. The city's finances were depleted by the annual tribute sent to Istanbul, as well as by the depredations of the Mamluks, who, having infiltrated the ranks of the janissaries, had access to customs revenues, and, by other means, to property taxes as well. Such corruption within the administration did not encourage major enterprises. Alexandria was marginalized because of a weak administration, which failed to maintain close links with Cairo.

The Ottoman sultans conquered Egypt in 1517. Selim I kept the existing institutions and appointed governors, who were under the control of the army and its redoubtable corps of janissaries.

The population of Alexandria shrank appreciably. Estimates for the total range from 3,000 to 15,000 inhabitants, the majority being Muslim and Coptic Egyptians, together with Turks, people from the Maghreb, Syrians, Jews, and a handful of Frankish merchants. Plague was the main cause of depopulation: Alexandria was to remain the hub of the disease right up to the 19th century.

Commercial activity

The sea route around the Cape of Good Hope was discovered in 1498, and Arab fleets in the Red Sea now came under attack from the Portuguese. In 1502, the caravels of the Portuguese admiral Pedro Álvares Cabral prevented spices from reaching the markets of Alexandria. Yet despite these problems, Alexandria remained one of Egypt's five customs posts, with authority over Rosetta and Abukir, and continued

to enjoy a modest prosperity through its maritime trade.

In 1517 the Venetians at once persuaded Selim to renew the treaties that had previously applied, and the French and Catalans soon followed: there was to be no poll tax and no property taxes (especially not on churches), consuls were to have sole jurisdiction over their nationals, there was to be freedom of movement,

‘Alexandria is an entrepôt dealing with a fair volume of trade. It is the gateway for all goods leaving Egypt in the direction of the Mediterranean, with the exception of rice from Damietta. Europeans have trading posts there, where agents barter our merchandise. You will always see vessels from Marseille, Livorno, Venice, Ragusa and the Papal States; but laying up there for the winter is dangerous. The new port, the only one where Europeans are allowed, has become so filled up with sand that during storms the vessels bump against the bottom with their keels; furthermore, as this bottom consists of rock, the anchor cables are often cut by the friction, and then one ship is dragged against another and pushes that against a third, and one after the other, they are all lost.’

Comte de Volnay
Voyage en Syrie et en Égypte, 1787

The harbour of Alexandria *c.* 1700.

and no restriction was to be imposed on the freedom to trade. The merchandise in question was the same as before, with silk, cotton, pepper, ginger, aromatics, gum arabic, natron and rice among the principal commodities exported. In the early 16th century coffee was introduced from the Yemen, and its consumption became widespread in the 18th century. In the early 17th century tobacco was introduced. The two new products had a tonic effect on economic activity, despite intermittent periods of crisis. The principal trade route was along the axis of Istanbul–Izmir–Alexandria. So much traffic was generated that Ottoman shipping was unable to cope, and most of the trade within the Ottoman Empire was conducted by European ships. The figures are impressive: in the course of 1782, 1,172 ships berthed at Alexandria, mostly from Istanbul, Tunis, Izmir and Salonica, but also from cities in western Europe.

Ottoman Alexandria was a diminished yet still relatively wealthy city. There was competition from Rosetta and Damietta, but no other Egyptian port could deal with as many ships as Alexandria. It comes as no surprise that Bonaparte chose it as the place from which to launch his Egyptian expedition.

The introduction of tobacco in the 17th century caused a considerable stir in Egyptian society, and even sparked brawls among some of the Maghrebians settled in the country. But its use spread rapidly, and a number of Ottoman pipes have been found in digs undertaken by the Centre for Alexandrian Studies. Seen here are an Ottoman pipe (opposite) and a fellah smoking (left).

In the 18th century the Mamluks, successful at infiltrating the Ottoman army and administration, became the real masters of the country. Murad Bey became their leader after the capture of Cairo in 1776.

Mohammed Ali brought about a renaissance in Egypt. An unlettered and unscrupulous Albanian, he proved an accomplished strategist and administrator, and led his country in military successes that threatened the authority of the sultan in Istanbul. His policy of cooperation with Europe encouraged the formation of an engineer class that was to be responsible for the building of modern Egypt.

CHAPTER 4
COSMOPOLITAN ALEXANDRIA

The bronze equestrian statue of Mohammed Ali by Alfred Jacquemart (right) looks down on the square that once bore his name in the heart of Alexandria, at the strategic and symbolic meeting point between the Turkish town and the European city (see p. 95). Opposite: the new Ramleh Boulevard.

Bonaparte's trumpets

When the people of Alexandria saw outlined on the horizon the sails of the 280 ships in the fleet commanded by Napoleon Bonaparte (1769–1821), they could not believe their eyes. On the evening of 1 July 1798 50,000 men led by no fewer than 32 generals, together with 1,200 horses and 170 cannon, were disembarked about 15 km (10 miles) west of Alexandria. During the night they advanced up to the walls, and then took the town after a few hours of fighting against weak opposition from Ottoman troops, supported by the local Bedouin. On the French side, some thirty men were dead and two generals were wounded.

Disappointment soon set in when they saw the state of Egypt's former capital. Bonaparte did not linger, but ordered a forced march to Cairo. That was where power resided and where the real confrontation would take place.

The purpose of the carefully planned expedition had been kept secret. The soldiers thought they were

Bonaparte disembarked on the coast near Alexandria, despite heavy seas. He was in a hurry to take the city, and the next day entered Alexandria. There he paid homage to the head of the military, Mohammed el-Koraim, for his bravery and presented him with a sword (opposite), confirming him in his position of governor.

heading for Cyprus, and only on the eve of disembarcation was an announcement by Bonaparte read out on board each ship: 'Glory to the sultan, glory to the French army, his friend. A curse on the Mamluks, and good fortune to the people of Egypt!'

The official purpose was to deliver the Egyptians from the Mamluks and to restore control to the Sublime Porte in Istanbul. It is true that a handful of French traders had been maltreated by the Mamluks, and the consul Magallon had borne the brunt. The Mamluk rulers Ibrahim and Murad Bey had systematically bled the country dry and ceased to answer to the sultan in Istanbul. The latter had sent a military expedition to regain the country, but it had been unsuccessful. Was that, however, conceivably an adequate reason for sending in a force of this magnitude? Clearly not, as the Ottoman Empire made plain when it condemned the invasion and declared *jihad* against France on 9 September.

Much ink has been expended on speculations as to the true reasons for the expedition: Bonaparte wanted to follow in Alexander the Great's footsteps, approach from Asia and take the Republic's enemies in the rear; the occupation of Egypt would threaten the route to

By the time of Bonaparte's arrival, Alexandria's mighty walls, which had so impressed early travellers, enclosed nothing grander than a few gardens. This view (below) is from the great *Description de l'Égypte*, published later by the expedition's team of scholars.

Bonaparte brought 160 scholars with him on his expedition to Egypt. The research they carried out formed the basis of the magnificent illustrated *Description de l'Égypte*, the first of whose twenty volumes was published in 1810. This drawing shows the group of *savants*.

India of the British, with whom France was at war; or it was an opportunity seized by the Directory to rid themselves for a time of a troublesome young general. The expedition encountered a number of setbacks, but it was to have a profound impact on the history of Egypt, and more particularly that of Alexandria.

While Bonaparte settled in Cairo, Desaix pursued Murad Bey into Upper Egypt as far as Philae, and the army launched a murderous campaign in Syria in pursuit of Ibrahim Bey, for three years Alexandria was transformed once again into a stronghold: Fort Napoleon, Fort Cafarelli and Fort Crétin are still a feature of the landscape today. The British were unable to take the town, but battles raged in the surrounding region.

Abukir, some 30 km (20 miles) east of Alexandria, was the site of no less than three battles. The first, the Battle of the Nile, took place at sea on 1 August 1798 when the British Admiral Nelson (1758–1805) finally located the French fleet, which Admiral Brueys thought he had safely concealed in the bay in the shelter of an

A bronze piece of the helm of Admiral Brueys' flagship, the *Dauphin Royal*, rechristened the *Orient* at the Revolution. Fragments of the wreck were recovered by underwater archaeologists at Abukir in 1984.

island. He had not reckoned with the daring of Nelson and his much more experienced sailors, who cut between the anchored French ships and the shore. It was a massacre; apart from a few craft that managed to escape, Bonaparte's entire fleet was sent to the bottom.

The following year, on 25 July 1799, a second battle was fought at Abukir. This time, Bonaparte led his troops to a brilliant victory over an Ottoman force twice the size of his own. Only a month later, however, Bonaparte embarked almost furtively at Alexandria for Toulon, leaving his generals behind, completely at a loss. Kléber took command at first, but he was assassinated in Cairo, and his successor Menou was a far less decisive personality. Menou lost the third battle of Abukir on 21 March 1801, at the gates of Alexandria, to British troops commanded by Sir Ralph Abercromby. The town capitulated on 2 September, and on 20 September the French expeditionary corps was forced out of Egypt, leaving behind all the antiquities that had been painstakingly collected.

Alexandria, where the military expedition had started, had been French for three years. Now it was here that the whole adventure drew to a sorry close, as the soldiers assembled to reembark. Alexandria may initially have disappointed them because of its small size; but it remained Egypt's gateway to the Mediterranean. Its strategic importance was not to be forgotten by the men who ruled Egypt in the decades to come.

After disembarking at Abukir on 21 March 1801 the British army won a famous victory against the troops commanded by the French general Menou. The British general, Abercromby (above), won the day but lost his life. England subsequently played a leading role in Egypt's development: although the British were repulsed by Mohammed Ali in 1807, their wish for control of the Mediterranean and, after 1869, for access to India via the Suez Canal led them to take over the running of the country, attempting to influence successive governments up to the nationalization of the Suez Canal in 1956.

Thanks to the efforts of the few French scholars and artists who remained in Alexandria, we have a wealth of documentation about the town. Two maps were drawn up, one a detailed plan, showing each individual lot, the other less detailed and including the surrounding area. The plates of the *Description de l'Égypte* show the town's principal monuments, the fort of Qaitbay (opposite, from a watercolour by Conté, a member of the expedition), the city walls, mosques, houses, and cisterns. The population too was described and recorded, to show its customs, skills and workforce (left, a sailor drawn by Dutertre). Antiquities were not forgotten: Cleopatra's Needles (the two obelisks erected by Augustus to mark the entrance to the Caesareum, the temple of the imperial cult), Pompey's Pillar, and the hypogea of the Necropolis. Descriptions and plates were devoted to the artefacts excavated, from small objects such as terracotta figures and scarabs to marble statues of Marcus Aurelius and Septimius Severus, found near the coast (now in the British Museum).

Mohammed Ali and the Alexandrian renaissance

Mohammed Ali was an Albanian from Kavala, a small Ottoman town 150 km (100 miles) northeast of Salonica. As a volunteer in the Ottoman army he took part in the battle of Abukir in 1799. After the departure of the French the struggle between the Ottoman authorities and the Mamluk beys intensified. Mohammed Ali played his cards well: at the head of the Albanian corps, he took Cairo from the Mamluks in 1804. The following year, he was given the title of pasha by the sultan in Istanbul, and in 1807 he defeated the English in the battle of Rosetta, putting paid to their ambitions of reconquest. Finally, in 1811, he invited the four hundred Mamluk leaders to a feast at his palace in the Citadel in Cairo, and massacred them all.

Mohammed Ali now began to develop a Mediterranean policy that brought rapid results, much to the discomfort of the European powers and the increasingly insecure Turkish government. He also reorganized the Egyptian administration, nationalized

Mohammed Ali received official guests at his palace of Ras el-Tin, built in 1817. Here he is welcoming an English delegation, among them the painter David Roberts. The view out to the busy western port is a reminder of his expansionist policies.

The harem of the Ras el-Tin Palace was photographed in daguerreotype in 1839 by the painter Horace Vernet, in the presence of a rapt Mohammed Ali, who is said to have exclaimed, 'It's the work of the devil!' The image was later reproduced as a print (opposite, above).

land, and planned new dams and major irrigation projects on the Nile. Once again Egypt was under the control of a tyrannical centralized authority.

Mohammed Ali greatly admired Bonaparte and France, and he called in French engineers to oversee his construction schemes and summoned French experts to reform his armies. He also sent Egyptians to study in Paris. The country unexpectedly blossomed, and people talked of an Egyptian renaissance.

In Alexandria, nothing had improved under the French occupation – the streets were still dirt tracks. But under Mohammed Ali, in the 1820s, a genuine urban environment began to take shape.

To demonstrate his attachment to the town, Mohammed Ali chose it in 1817 as the site for his palace, on the western tip of the island of Pharos. With its fine views over the sea, this symbolized his desire to renew Egypt's links with the Mediterranean world, an aspiration that the country's rulers had lost sight of since medieval times. He soon found the means to implement his new policy, and Alexandria, where he spent increasing amounts of his time, played a key role. Major engineering works were begun without delay. The engineer Pascal Coste was put in charge of scouring and restoring the canal: with a forced-labour team consisting of as many as 200,000 *fellaheen*, he cleared the channel of the ancient canal and extended it to meet the Rosetta branch of the Nile, producing a waterway 2.70 m (8.5 feet) deep. Officially opened in 1821 and named the Mahmoudiya Canal after Sultan Mahmud, it provided the town for the first time in five centuries with a regular supply of drinking water, as well as a permanently navigable route by which vessels could enter the western harbour. Transport links with the rest of the country and in particular the capital were improved beyond measure, and journey times reduced. Instead of the

The engineer Pascal Coste was entrusted with major civil engineering projects such as the restoration of the Mahmoudiya Canal, which was designed to improve communications between Cairo and Alexandria and to ensure a regular supply of drinking water for the latter (bottom: his plan for a lock between the canal and the Nile). Coste also erected a telegraph line between Alexandria and Cairo, enabling news to reach the pasha in only fifteen minutes.

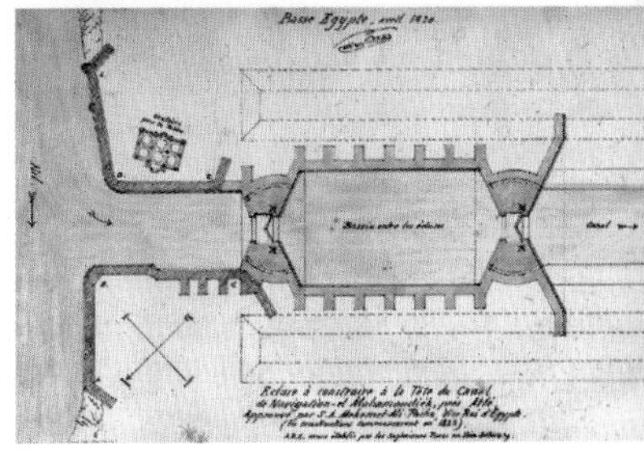

Ecluse à construire à la Tête du Canal de Navigation-el Mahamoudieh, près Atfé. Approuvé par S.A. Mehemet-Ali-Pacha, Vice Roi d'Egypte. (les constructions commenceront en 1823). A.B.C. murs établis par les Ingénieurs Turcs en Juin-Juillet 1819.

week it once took to get to Cairo, three days were now sufficient.

Mohammed Ali did not envisage a peaceful future for Egypt, and so he began to build new walls on the site of the Tulunid fortifications. This proved a pointless activity: Colonel Galice Bey later estimated it would require a minimum of 25,000 men to defend them (not, he added, that that was *his* problem). In 1860 they began to be dismantled, and all that remains today are a few traces near the Shallalat Gardens.

On the banks of the Mahmoudiya Canal stood the villas of rich Alexandrians and one of the royal palaces (Palace No. 3). Here residents could enjoy an atmosphere of rural calm, and stroll down a famous promenade known as the 'Champs Élysées'.

Under the new Mediterranean strategy, Alexandria urgently needed to expand the capacity of its harbour. In 1829 Mohammed Ali commissioned the French engineers Cerisy and Mougel to construct a large dock in the western port, which, after more than a millennium, was reopened to Christian shipping. He also undertook to build the first ever Egyptian fleet. Together, the shipyard and the fleet employed a force of some 20,000 men.

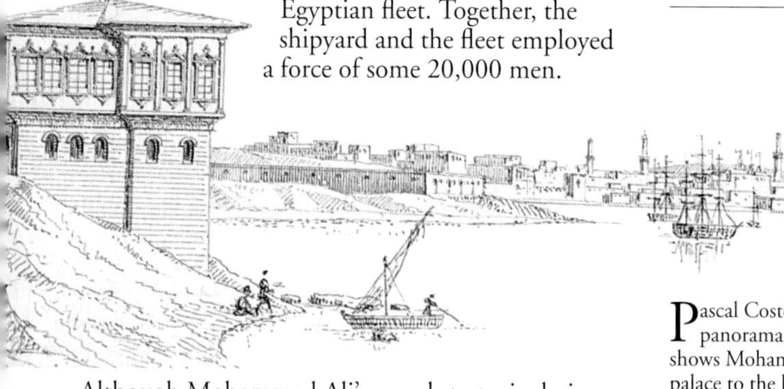

Pascal Coste's panorama of 1819 shows Mohammed Ali's palace to the left, the city wall beyond it, and to the right the hills of Kom el-Dick and Kom el-Nadura, Pompey's Pillar, and Fort Qaitbay.

Although Mohammed Ali's grand strategic designs were soon to be proved unrealistic (the combined Ottoman and Egyptian fleet was defeated at Navarino in 1827), his modernization initiatives had spectacular effects on trade that he had never foreseen: the number

The port of Alexandria, seen here *c.* 1870, grew steadily during the 19th century. In the course of 1822, 900 ships anchored there; two years later the number had risen to 1,290, and by the 1860s the annual figure was 2,000.

of ships docking annually in Alexandria increased from 1,092 in 1830 to 1,607 in 1850, and from 2,137 in 1880 to 6,700 in 1905, when 4 million barrels of merchandise passed through the port.

As trade increased, and immigrants flocked to this new El Dorado, the size of the city's population grew: it rocketed from 13,000 in 1821 to 60,000 in 1838, 180,000 in 1860, 232,000 just twenty years later, and 573,000 in 1927. Egyptians came there from all over the country. While there had only been a handful of foreigners in the city when Mohammed Ali took over, gradually they came to form a substantial proportion of the population: census returns record 14.5 per cent in 1897 and 19 per cent in 1907. The figures given in the census of 1907 are 359,911 Egyptians, 25,393 Greeks, 17,860 Italians, 10,658 British, and 8,556 French.

'I counted up to twenty-one French flags; the Sardinian navy was much in evidence in the port of Alexandria, as it is in all the other ports of the Mediterranean; we saw many Greek ships, ships from Livorno, Trieste, Malta, the Pasha's fleet. . . . Most of the European vessels come in to take on cotton, broad beans and other produce from Egypt; they bring in iron, copper, cloth, wood for use in shipbuilding, weapons and clothing for the soldiers, and every kind of machine and utensil of which the Pasha's manufacturing industry might have need.'

Joseph Michaud, historian, 1829

Foreigners were free to use the streets of Alexandria for community events. Here the French colony celebrates the Feast of the Assumption in 1866, moving in formal procession through the city to the Catholic church.

The European city

Mohammed Ali encouraged foreigners to settle in Egypt, especially Greeks and Syrians from the Ottoman Empire. He gave them their own areas of the city, inside the deserted walls. Ultimately, the population of the Attarine and Mancheyya quarters was to be 30 or 40 per cent foreign. This is where the European city developed, around the Place des Consuls, laid out in 1834 to the design of the Italian architect Francesco Mancini. Initially a parade ground, in 1860 it was transformed into a garden square and renamed Place Mohamed Ali, after the bronze equestrian statue of the pasha in the middle (this provoked hostile demonstrations whipped up by the religious authorities, who thought displaying the ruler's image was contrary to Islamic beliefs).

Francesco Mancini was the head of Ornato, a committee set up in 1834 to oversee urban planning. A city with broad straight avenues and vast squares gradually took shape, extending progressively eastwards. This was where the rich Greek merchants chose to make their homes, in an environment of

large villas set in private gardens. As expansion continued the walls were taken down, and suburbs extended out towards Rushdy and Ramleh. With the increased distances to be covered, there was a compelling need for a railway system to serve the city, and Ramleh station was built in 1860.

The municipal council of Alexandria was formally constituted in 1890: on it served Egyptian notables, often of Ottoman origin, members of the leading Coptic families, and representatives of the foreign communities. Using the revenue from local taxes, its fourteen committees ran the city, overseeing the water supply, drainage, street paving, and urban projects in general (port, warehouses, construction of the Corniche from 1905 onwards). The experiment was the envy of every other city in the country. It continued in being for half a century, until corruption and a confusion of powers led to its demise in 1935.

The architects employed were mostly Italian and Greek, with names including Avoscani, Lasciac, Loria and Paraskevas. Some quarters of Alexandria took on a distinctly Neapolitan air. As tastes moved on, the choice lay between Art Deco, neoclassical (used for the villas of the Greek cotton merchants), neo-Byzantine (apartment blocks on the Corniche), neo-pharaonic (the Polytechnic), neo-Renaissance, even Fascist colonial (the Italian school). Buildings were often expressions of national sentiment. A few architects of European distinction were employed; one of Auguste Perret's villas survives today.

‘The square called the Place des Consuls [below] would grace any of our finest cities. The square is in fact a large rectangle, surrounded

by consulates and the houses of rich European businessmen; four rows of trees form a magnificent avenue down the middle; fountains play into two basins at either end of this attractive promenade, providing a refreshing coolness; and finally, the vast building of the Egyptian Bank at the end completes the view.’

C. David, 1865

Alexandria is a repository of buildings in different architectural styles: these neo-Byzantine (opposite below) and neo-Venetian (left) apartment buildings were designed by the Italian architect Loria in the 1920s.

HEAD QUARTERS
BRITISH GARRISON

In the early 20th century, Rue Fuad (opposite), the Place des Consuls or Place Mohamed Ali, with its equestrian statue of Mohammed Ali (left), and Rue Chérif Pacha (below) formed the bustling heart of the European city. Among the horsedrawn carriages, Alexandrians appear dressed in an assortment of European clothes and *djellibiyahs*. The common form of headgear is the *tarboosh* (the Egyptian fez), which was worn by all civil servants up to 1952.

The position of foreigners

The diversity of Alexandrian commerce is reflected in the six advertisements on these pages. Anticlockwise from the top, they are for a photographer, motor tyres, cigarettes, a tailor, a jeweller, and novelties.

Foreigners were for the most part engaged in commerce, in the importation of industrial machinery, or in construction work. The export trade consisted of agricultural products, notably cotton when it was in short supply during the American Civil War from 1860: the drop in American sales created a boom in Egypt, followed by sudden collapse. Foreigners were also employed in administration and in the mixed tribunals that were set up to adjudicate in disputes between foreign nationals and local people.

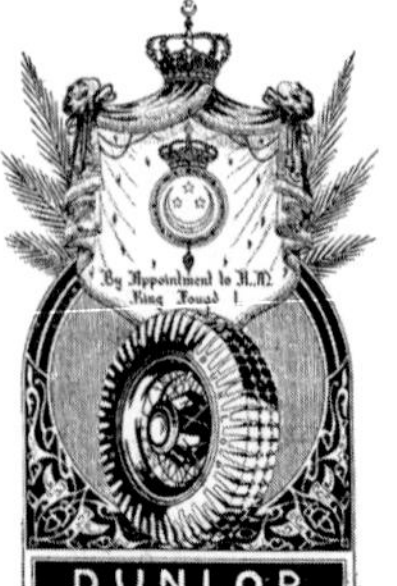

Disagreements between two foreigners were dealt with directly by the consuls, who retained considerable power.

Foreigners did not pay taxes, and their houses were sacrosanct – something that could cause problems, notably when they refused to pay rent owed to local landlords. There were foreign postal services almost everywhere – English, German, Austrian, Italian and French. The latter, set up in 1836, printed French postal markers and then stamps, which continued to bear the name of the city right up to 1931.

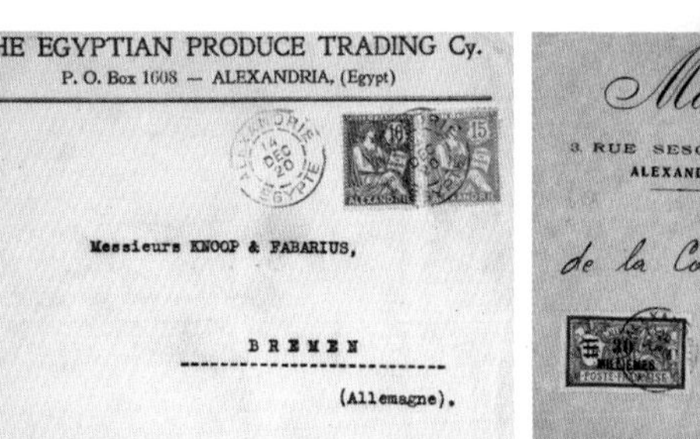

The three envelopes above, addressed to Bremen, Paris and Genoa and franked in Alexandria, are reminders of the city's flourishing foreign trade.

The traffic in antiquities was a profitable business, too. Drovetti, who was French consul from 1804, ventured into this lucrative trade with the active support of Mohammed Ali. The pasha, it must be said, had not the slightest concern for his country's heritage. He even suggested to the engineer Linant de Bellefonds that the

Fabrique de Cigarettes Egyptiennes
COUTARELLI FRÈRES
FONDÉE EN 1890
CHAMPS ELYSÉES – ALEXANDRIE – MOHARREM BEY
Téléphones : Direction 3190 · Fabrique 5309

pyramids be demolished in order to build a dam across the Nile. The Frenchman had to convince him that this would be far more expensive than obtaining the necessary stone from a quarry before he would give up the idea. Alexandria certainly suffered from his lack of interest, and before long found itself stripped of its few antiquities of any note: the obelisks known as Cleopatra's Needles were presented by the pasha to England and America; one departed for the banks of the Thames in 1877, while the other went to New York in 1879.

LES PLUS GRANDS MAGASINS DE NOUVEAUTES DE TOUT L'ORIENT
S. & S. SEDNAOUI & Co. Ltd.
ALEXANDRIE
Rue Sidi-El-Metwalli, près le Caracol Anglais

•The true Alexandrian is a businessman, never mind what sort of business. Money, that's what he's after. Always on the lookout, he jots down columns of figures on his cigarette box, advances, feints, conceals his intentions under a flow of badinage, extricates himself from the inextricable with amazing mobility, blows hot and cold, always, as they say, "leaves the door open," settles for less if he must, and, finally, knows how to walk away from a bankruptcy unscathed.•

Fernand Leprette
1939

MAISON DE CONFIANCE
ZIVY FRÈRES & Co.
JOAILLIERS DE S. M. LE ROI

The communities

Nationalities such as Greeks, Italians, Armenians and Syrian-Lebanese tended to remain within their own groups, where they had language and religion in common. To supplement the consular authorities, each community elected representatives to look after its members' interests and to help the needy. The community would own land, sometimes whole quarters of the city, the income from which was used to finance common enterprises (schools, places of worship, hospitals, theatres, clubs, newspapers) and to care for the underprivileged (orphanages and old peoples' homes).

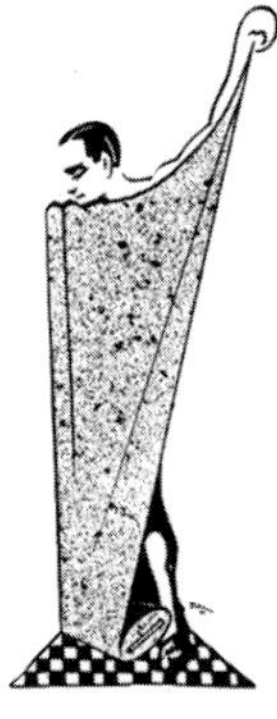

GH. PAPAZIAN
TAILLEUR POUR HOMMES
10, Rue Sesostris ALEXANDRIE 10, Rue Sesostris

The city's villas reflect the taste and the wealth of a select group of Alexandrians. Opposite, above left: the staircase of the girls' school presented by the Greek philanthropist Averoff to his community.
Opposite, below: the bathroom of the villa of an Egyptian royal princess, decorated with tiles and stained glass from Nancy.
Opposite, above right, and this page: staircase, dining room and Oriental Saloon of the Villa Cordahi, built for the Kaiser's visit in 1901.

'The long beautiful reception-rooms had been pierced with alcoves and unexpected corners to increase their already great seating-capacity and sometimes as many as two or three hundred guests sat down to elaborate and meaningless dinners – observing their host lost in the contemplation of a rose lying upon an empty plate before him.'

Lawrence Durrell
Justine, 1957

A number of Ottoman subjects, especially Syrian-Lebanese, Jews and Armenians, became attached to one or other of the foreign communities, and received protection from them, either by virtue of their occupation or for services rendered. This arrangement was much sought after, because it meant you avoided taxes. It could lead to some curious anomalies. Many Jews, for instance, were associated with the Italian community. When news got out that there had been a fire in the archives at Livorno, numbers of them went to the consular authorities in Alexandria and asked for 'replacements' of their papers. In a trice, they became Italian citizens. When a Fascist consul was sent by Mussolini to sort out his compatriots in Alexandria, he was most surprised to find a large Jewish contingent, with little enthusiasm for the antisemitic policies of the Duce.

'The Alexandrian goes from his office to the Exchange [above], thinks of nothing but his financial schemes . . . The Exchange, like the god Moloch, has lost count of its victims.'
Fernand Leprette, 1939

The Jewish community had half a dozen synagogues, a hospital, learned and philanthropic societies, religious schools, and secular institutions like the free schools founded in 1885 by Baron Behor de Menasce (below).

The Turkish town

Out on the peninsula, the Turkish town was still there, with its narrow lanes and overhanging houses. The population was almost exclusively Egyptian, with a density of more than 50,000 per sq km (130,000 per square mile), compared with 20,000 (51,800 per square mile) in the European city. The old crafts flourished, but taxation was crippling. There were effectively two towns side by side that were largely unaware of each another. Few Europeans ventured into the Turkish town; few even knew it existed. Travellers with a taste for the exotic saw in Alexandria only the European city,

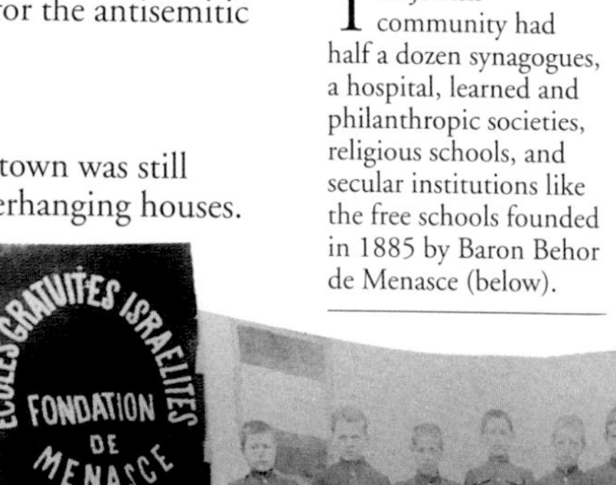

and could not wait to leave for Cairo. This explains why there are so many paintings of the capital and so few of Alexandria.

The bombardment of 1882

The cumulative cost of the excavation of the Suez Canal (opened in 1869), of large-scale urban developments in Cairo, and of lavish entertainments, combined with general financial extravagance, led to the deposition of Ismail Pasha, who had been Khedive of Egypt from 1863 to 1879, and his exile in Istanbul. Egypt was bankrupt. In 1876, a Franco-British condominium took control of the economy. The result was a surge of nationalism, which was exploited by General Arabi Pasha. As defence minister, he took a stand against foreign domination and armed the forts of Alexandria. The response was immediate: the British fleet bombarded the city, hitting with pinpoint accuracy both Fort Qaitbay and Place Mohamed Ali.

The Turkish town, founded in 1517, soon grew to occupy the whole of the isthmus north of the medieval city. Its narrow streets were made to feel even narrower by overhanging upper storeys. Small-scale industry and trade occupied shops, bazaars and workshops. Here the Egyptian population lived, and among them some Jews and Greeks. Surrounded by its colourful bustle, with the smells of spices and pastourma, the cries of men wielding handcarts, and the stalls blocking your way, you felt very remote from the European city, even though that was just a few streets away.

Following riots in the city (above, an execution during the uprisings of 1881), the British fleet bombarded Alexandria in 1882. Directly in the line of fire was Fort Qaitbay, which was almost totally destroyed (left, the entrance). The Place Mohamed Ali and the area around it (opposite below, the Italian Post Office) were reduced to rubble. Ironically, so too was the British Consulate (opposite, above). Skirmishes ensued; some foreigners were lynched, and buildings were looted and burned. The British cracked down hard. Arabi's army was defeated in the Delta, and the Egyptian Government was made to compensate the owners of buildings that had been destroyed, an arrangement that was much abused. The great square was soon rebuilt more splendid than ever.

Rediscovering Alexandria's past

The Greco-Roman Museum was founded in 1892 to house items presented by local notables. Its collections were later expanded as a result of excavations conducted between 1892 and 1963 by the Italian archaeologists Giuseppe Botti, Evaristo Breccia and Achille Adriani.

Alexandria suffered from bad timing as far as archaeology was concerned, because the rapid expansion of the city under Mohammed Ali took place before the era of the great archaeological investigations in the Mediterranean. The centre of the European city, which overlay the heart of the ancient city, was built up in the 1830s–50s (and then remained untouched for a century and a half). The first scholarly archaeological institution concerned with ancient Greece, the French School in Athens, was not founded until 1846.

Excavations were attempted, most notably by D. G. Hogarth, who was despatched from the British School of Archaeology in Athens, founded in 1885. But what was there left to find in Alexandria? When in 1894 Hogarth dug down into the mound of shards called Kom el-Dick, at a depth of over 10 m (33 ft) he found a few late Roman levels. In 1889, the famous Heinrich Schliemann, eager to add the Tomb of Alexander to his list of discoveries following his dazzling successes at Mycenae and Troy, had been similarly disappointed. The leading institutions all gave up on Alexandria, and sent their teams of archaeologists instead to Asia Minor and other more promising areas of the Near East.

While the centre had been modernized, however, the outskirts were still untouched, since Mohammed Ali had banned building outside the walls. Archaeologists therefore turned their attention to the cemeteries,

Athènes 4 janvier 1889.

Je partage parfaitement votre opinion que le Sôma doit se trouver dans les environs immédiats de la Mosquée du prophète Daniel, laquelle couvre probablement le site exact du tombeau d'Alexandre. Très vraisemblablement le Mnéma ou tombeau de Cleopatre et de Marc Antoine faisait aussi partie du Sôma.

H Schliemann

The founder of the Greco-Roman Museum, Giuseppe Botti, is seen here (in the foreground, wearing a tarboosh) in the courtyard of a large tomb in the Karmuz district. He was responsible for some major discoveries, including the catacombs of Kom es-Shoqafa and the Sarapeum. He and his successors produced many reports and fine reference journals such as the *Bulletin* of the Société Royale d'Archéologie (now Société Archéologique) of Alexandria, which is still published today.

where they had to compete with people bent on using the ancient sites as quarries. This was the background against which the brilliant excavations of the German archaeologist Ernst von Sieglin were carried out; he went on to produce exemplary publications on the catacombs of Kom es-Shoqafa and an excellent book on the necropolises.

Von Sieglin was the exception, however. Alexandrian archaeology was otherwise to be undertaken only by local scholars without any international backing. Scientifically they were people of the highest quality, but the means they had at their disposal were modest. A map of the ancient city had been drawn up as early as 1866 by the engineer Mahmud al-Falaki, on the order of the Khedive Ismail: the khedive wanted to

Opposite: a note from Heinrich Schliemann, dated 4 January 1889, from his correspondence with the director of the Greco-Roman Museum and local scholars about the Tomb of Alexander. He writes: 'I completely share your view that the Soma [i.e. Tomb] must lie in the immediate vicinity of the mosque of the Prophet Daniel, which probably stands on the exact site of the Tomb of Alexander. In all probability, the Mnema or Tomb of Cleopatra and Mark Antony also formed part of the Soma.'

help his friend Napoleon III, who was writing a biography of Caesar and needed to be able to describe the setting of the war in Alexandria. El-Falaki sank some two hundred exploratory shafts, and the result was that Alexandrian archaeology had an accurate map for use in future research.

Among the researchers who followed were Dr Neroutsos, a medical doctor, who was interested in topography and epigraphy, and after him an Italian, Giuseppe Botti (d. 1903), who persuaded the city council to establish the Greco-Roman Museum in 1892. For more than half a century he and his successors at the museum, the Italians Evaristo Breccia and Achille Adriani, pursued the project of rescuing the Alexandrian heritage, working tirelessly and publishing many works of reference.

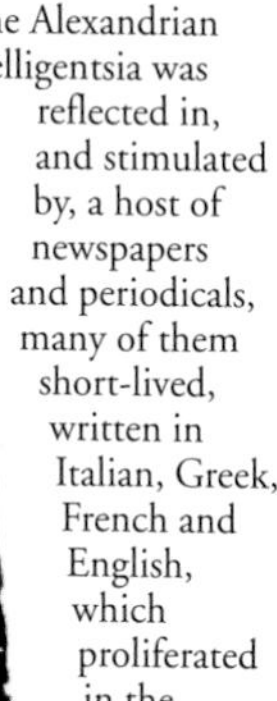

The cultural life of the Alexandrian intelligentsia was reflected in, and stimulated by, a host of newspapers and periodicals, many of them short-lived, written in Italian, Greek, French and English, which proliferated in the decades around 1900.

A cultural mosaic

As the size of the urban population increased, there was a parallel growth in recreational activities for the various social classes. Some of these activities took place within individual communities, and were based on the particular community's language or religion. Other pastimes attracted members of the intelligentsia from all the different groupings – local Egyptians and Ottomans, and Muslim, Jewish and Christian foreign nationals. At the same time a purely Egyptian culture was evolving, often unsuspected by foreigners, which achieved particular distinction in the realms of music, sculpture, architecture, film and literature.

Language and religion were the bases on which Alexandria was divided into different cultural communities, each of which received support from a foreign government or from patrons. The French State, for example, contributed to the needs of the Lycée Français, whereas the Greek schools were funded privately by rich cotton merchants such as the Tossitsa, Salvago, Averoff and Benaki families. German, English, Armenian, French, Italian and Jewish schools existed side by side.

Sarah Bernhardt
à Alexandrie

The Salvago Theatre was one of the Greek community's cultural haunts, as the Alliance Française was for the French. Talent was appreciated and encouraged within the community as a means of giving expression to its concerns and aspirations. There was an explosion of literary activity, in the form of newspapers and countless periodicals – literary, historical, political – some of high quality, written in all the many

‘There are two main clubs, the Khedival and the Mohammed Ali. These clubs offer a remarkable level of comfort. They are richly and luxuriously appointed, have rooms for gaming and for billiards, a café, a restaurant, rooms for reading, writing, and conversation. Every morning they receive the political dispatches from the previous day [above, a postcard caricature of the announcement of an Allied victory in 1916] and the latest news from the Exchange. They are of invaluable assistance and rare usefulness for all those who want to be kept up to date with the arts and sciences, literary and dramatic movements, important events, the topics of the day, or for anyone who just wants to read.’

Louis Malosse
1896

languages spoken in Alexandria. Newspapers were legion, in Greek, Armenian, English and French, typical among them *Le Phare d'Alexandrie*, *La Réforme* and *Tachydromos*. Lectures were held on a variety of historical and literary subjects, and the fine arts were catered to by several art schools.

Μέρες τοῦ 1901

Τοῦτο εἰς αὐτὸν ὑπῆρχε τὸ ξεχωριστό,
ποὺ μέσα σ' ὅλην του τὴν ἔκλυσι
καὶ τὴν πολλήν του πεῖραν ἔρωτος,
παρ' ὅλην τὴν συνειθισμένη του
στάσεως καὶ ἡλικίας ἐναρμόνισιν,
ἐτύχαιναν στιγμὲς — πλὴν βέβαια
σπανιότατες — ποὺ τὴν ἐντύπωσιν
ἔδιδε σάρκας σχεδὸν ἀθίκτου.

Τῶν εἴκοσι ἐννιά του χρόνων ἡ ἐμορφιά,
ἡ τόσο ἀπὸ τὴν ἡδονὴ δοκιμασμένη,
ἦσαν στιγμὲς ποὺ θύμιζε παράδοξα
ἔφηβο ποὺ — κάπως ἀδέξια — στὴν ἀγάπη
πρώτη φορὰ τὸ ἁγνό του σῶμα παραδίδει.

Κ. Π. Καβάφης

Constantine Cavafy was born in Alexandria and spent part of his childhood in England. After his return, he worked as a clerk in the Irrigation Service. He had his poems printed privately, and circulated them among his friends. His poetry often has an Alexandrian setting, whether the ancient city – not in its heyday but during its decadence or at moments of defeat ('God abandons Antony') – or the modern city, as in 'Days of 1901' (above).

A literary melting pot

Some talents were exceptional, although it often took the perspective of history for them to be recognized beyond their national circle. The poet Constantine Cavafy (1863–1933) was an exception: his subtle artistry won immediate praise in 1917 from E. M. Forster (1879–1970), who translated several of his poems, and was commended by Lawrence Durrell thirty years later, at a time when he was still far from achieving the enormous popularity he enjoys today. Yet Forster wrote in *Pharos and Pharillon* (1923): 'Such a writer can never be popular. He flies both too slowly and too high. . . . He has the strength (and of course the limitations) of the recluse, who, though not afraid of the world, always stands at a slight angle to it . . .'

Stratis Tsirkas, in his trilogy *Drifting Cities*, tells of the divisions within the Greek community during the Second World War, as Communists served with the Greek troops in the battle of El Alamein, while the Greek king and his government had fled German-occupied Athens and taken refuge in Cairo. Giuseppe Ungaretti in his early poems describes his vision of the desert and the city, while Fausta Cialente paints a picture of life in the Italian Fascist community before the Second World War. If Alexandria was a literary melting pot, this was because of its intellectual climate and multicultural influences, the quality of the education there, and the sense it offered of living in a historic city.

Foreigners, real foreigners that is, resident for just a few months or a few years, have sometimes been able to capture the peculiar atmosphere of Alexandria. That was certainly the case with E. M. Forster, a Red Cross volunteer in 1915, whose two guides to the city are masterpieces of wit and fine description, covering both the city's ancient history and its multicultural present. And it is most notably true of Lawrence Durrell (1912–90), posted as an attaché in the city during the Second World War, who made it the subject of his great series of novels – *Justine*, *Balthazar*, *Mountolive* and *Clea* – that together form the *Alexandria Quartet* (1957–60).

Lawrence Durrell sketched by Clea Badaro, the model for one of the heroines in the *Alexandria Quartet*.

'Everything about her person is honey-gold . . . The calmly disposed hands have a deftness and shapeliness which one only notices when one sees them at work, holding a paint-brush perhaps . . .'

Justine, 1957

A European social life

French was quickly adopted as the common language of the different communities. This *lingua franca* was taught in the state schools and at the Jesuit College up to the First World War; after that, the offspring of Alexandrian high society were educated in a number of schools run by French monks and nuns, and at the French Lycée. The English Girls' School and Victoria College were educationally just as sound, but initially they were a less obvious choice in a world where French was the accepted language. Their prestige and success grew, however, especially from the 1930s on.

Alexandria's Christian schools were popular with members of all communities. Teaching a French curriculum, they attracted the children of the Muslim, Christian and Jewish élites. Here we see an official reception at the Collège Ste-Catherine: a sister wearing a high winged coif greets an admiral and the French consul, on the occasion of a visit to the city by a ship of the French fleet.

Alexandrian society met at a number of different events. There was the theatre, where visiting French companies were welcomed; if the visitors were the Comédie Française, you could guarantee a full house. At the Opera, it was the Italian repertoire that always drew the most enthusiastic response. There were also countless concerts and lectures – at the Greco-Roman Museum, at the Société Royale d'Archéologie, or at the arts circle known as the Atelier. Eminent writers like Jean Cocteau and André Gide would sometimes put in an appearance, but just as with music, it was the popular writers that the Alexandrians really took to their hearts.

A very fashionable meeting place was the cinema. This form of entertainment grew with amazing speed: on 6 November 1896 the Lumière brothers came to Alexandria, just one year after their first public film-showings in Paris, and caused a sensation when audiences were able to see a film of a train arriving in Ramleh station,

The anniversary of the king's coronation was an opportunity for celebration. In 1929 (opposite, below), King Fuad invited the city's various official bodies to attend an open-air banquet in the gardens bequeathed to the city by Sir John Antoniadis, a Greek from Chios.

Osman Pasha Orphi

Requests the honour of

Mrs Cavafy & Sons

company at a Fête Champêtre at his villa on the banks of the Mahmoudieh Canal on Monday the 18th instant (Sham-el-Nesseem)

An invitation from Osman Pasha Orphi requesting the presence of the Cavafy family at a reception at his villa by the Mahmoudiya Canal.

which had been shot during the day and then developed and projected on the same evening. After that cinemas mushroomed in every quarter of the city. Alas, the Alhambra, the Majestic and the Cosmos that once stood in the centre disappeared under pressure from developers, but there are others that still survive as a reminder of this explosion of enthusiasm for the movies: there is the wonderful Metro, for example, a vast cinema built in 1950 in a modernistic style combining aluminium, wood and mosaic. Film magazines proliferated – among them *Cinégraphe-Journal* (which began publishing in 1913), *Ciné-Globe* (1931), and *Ciné-Images*. The Alexandrians' appetite for the cinema has continued unabated for a century or more. Even now, in the days of satellite television and video, it shows no sign of slackening.

Some of the films distributed by Universal Pictures for release in Alexandria's cinemas during the 1952–3 season.

A new Egyptian culture

Youssef Chahine, one of Egypt's most celebrated film directors, was born in Alexandria of a Syrian father and Greek mother. Many of his films are set in his native city. *Adieu Bonaparte* is concerned with the Napoleonic conquest, and *Alexandria, Why?* with the fate of the Jews; the still above is from *Alexandria Again and Forever.*

Alongside the imported art and entertainments laid on for the foreign communities, Egyptian creativity flourished in Alexandria, in working-class areas such as Kom el-Dick, where Sayyed Darwiche, the father of modern Egyptian music and writer of the national anthem, was born. His fame lives on even now, among people who have probably never heard of wonderfully talented painters such as Mahmud Said (1897–1964), or Mohammed Nagui and his sister Effat Nagui, who, although working in a Western tradition, nevertheless brought something distinctively Alexandrian to their works, as did the brothers Adham and Seif Wanly, with their small formats and subtle colours.

The equestrian statue of Mohammed Ali had been made in Paris in 1860 by the sculptor Alfred Jacquemart; the modern statue of the nationalist leader Saad Zaghlul, on the other hand, which looks down over the square named after him, is the work of an Egyptian sculptor, Mahmud Mukhtar.

Times had changed. Egyptians colonized the world of film, notably the director Mohammed Bayumi from the 1930s onwards, and from the 1950s Youssef

Many Alexandrian painters trained at the École des Beaux-Arts in Paris, but on their return home they produced original works, full of distinctively Egyptian life and colour. The subjects might be episodes from the city's glorious past, as in *The Scholars at the Museum*, a vast painting by Mohammed Nagui in the city council's function room; or urban landscapes, like *The Corniche of Alexandria by Night* by Mahmud Said (opposite, below); or scenes of social life like the dimly lit *Dancers* by the same artist (left). Their talents were fostered by an academy of arts, a vital artistic circle, the Atelier, and a Museum of Fine Arts with extensive collections. There are now a number of museums, like those in Cairo devoted to the works of Mohammed Nagui and Mahmud Mukhtar and the Museum of Modern Art, and the Mahmud Said Museum in Alexandria, that give a good idea of the richness and originality of these 20th-century Alexandrian painters and sculptors.

Chahine, who celebrated his birthplace in a number of films, among them *Alexandria, Why?* (1978) and *Alexandria Again and Forever* (1990). Alexandria was also the birthplace of the architect Hassan Fathy, author of the influential *Architecture for the Poor: An Experiment in Rural Egypt* (1973); several of his works can be seen near Agami beach. Last but not least, Egypt now boasts such distinguished writers in Arabic as Edwar Al-Kharrat, whose *City of Saffron* (1986) gives a moving account of life in Alexandria, and the 1988 Nobel prizewinner Naguib Mahfouz, the father of Egyptian social realism.

Alexandria now has more than three million inhabitants, plus another million Cairenes during the summer months. To this figure must be added the population of the unauthorized, often temporary, settlements to the east and west, as well as the many commuters who pile into the town in minibuses and packed trains. The result is a vast agglomeration extending ribbonlike between sea and lake for some 60 km (40 miles).

CHAPTER 5

ALEXANDRIA TODAY

The Corniche (opposite), 18 km (11 miles) long, links the port with the former royal palace of Montazah. Symbolic of the modern city's ties with the past, the new Library (right), with its circular roof, takes shape. It occupies a site facing the sea, close to that of the original Library.

Until 1914 Egypt remained an Ottoman province, governed by a semi-independent viceroy under what became known as a 'veiled' protectorate. In 1914 the umbilical cord with Istanbul was finally severed. Egypt would soon acquire a royal family, but in the meantime the 'veil' was lifted from British domination

and a protectorate proclaimed. 1919 saw a surge of nationalism. In Alexandria, protests became a part of everyday life, with big demonstrations led by Saad Zaghlul. In 1922, under pressure from unrest and strikes, the British proclaimed Egyptian independence; but it was a very limited form of independence, as Britain retained control over the Suez Canal, the army and the economy. From Fuad (viceroy from 1917, installed as king in 1922) to Farouk, power was contested between the British, the king, and the country's new political movements.

The king and the government continued to spend the summer in Alexandria, which was spoken of as 'the second capital'; but decisions were now taken in Cairo. True, war restored to the city some of its strategic importance. In the First World War, it acted as a reception post for the wounded from the Dardanelles (Alexandria's military cemeteries are full of their bodies), but it was far removed from the actual combat. During the Second World War, on the other hand, the front was much closer, and in October 1942 the guns could be heard at

Demonstrations against the British occupying power began after the First World War. In 1919 the protests were led by the nationalist hero Saad Zaghlul, who was exiled to Malta and then the Seychelles. His nationalist party, the Wafd, fought for independence, which was officially proclaimed in 1922; but real independence had yet to be achieved (left, demonstrators in Place Mohamed Ali in 1930; below, on Ramleh Boulevard in the 1930s). Today a bronze statue of Saad Zaghlul by the famous sculptor Mahmud Mukhtar stands in one of the city's largest squares. Symbolically, he gazes out to sea, indicating with a gesture of his hand Alexandria's Mediterranean destiny.

El Alamein, 100 km (60 miles) away. Indeed, Rommel all but succeeded in destroying the Allied ring around Alexandria – a situation to which some Egyptians (not to mention the Italian and German communities) would not have been averse.

But for the Alexandrians, times had already begun to change: in 1937, the Montreux Accords put an end to mixed tribunals and to the privileged status of foreigners. The country was reverting to its true owners, and Egypt had achieved independence. There was a strong sense that British occupation could not continue indefinitely.

In 1936 a large force of British ships occupied the western port (above). They were joined, in the course of the Second World War, by some of the French fleet. Although not officially at war, Alexandria became in effect an Allied garrison, creating a groundswell of support for the Axis powers, especially among the young officers of the Egyptian army.

From king to president

The postwar period was a time of recession, and of external crisis caused by the setting up of the state of Israel, with a first war in 1948, and an escalation of the conflict with the British on the banks of the Suez Canal. In 1952 Cairo was rocked by violent uprisings, following an attack by the British on a police post that had been infiltrated by terrorists. In the face of government impotence, a group of Free Officers, under the nominal leadership of General Neguib (although the true leader was Gamal Abdel Nasser), seized power on 23 July.

On 26 July, the action moved to Alexandria. King Farouk had succeeded his father Fuad in 1936, at the age of sixteen. An obese figure with a taste for the high life, he had become an unpopular ruler. Following the coup, the Free Officers had to decide his fate. Nasser was among those who ruled against trial and execution, and the king was forced to abdicate and sent into exile. From the palace built by Mohammed Ali at Ras el-Tin, Farouk embarked for Italy on the *Mahrousa*, which had

On 26 July 1952, King Farouk was forced to abdicate by the Free Officers who had staged a *coup d'état* three days earlier. One of Farouk's passions was fast sports cars, always red – the colour reserved for his exclusive use. Times had changed by the time of this photograph (above), where he is shown trying to hide behind his hand, as a black saloon ferries him to the western port.

been built by the Khedive Ismail to celebrate the opening of the Suez Canal.

26 July became the date on which the city annually celebrated its liberation, and on that day in 1956 Nasser delivered a marathon speech from the balcony of the Exchange. Suddenly he burst out laughing and announced to the astonished crowd of 250,000 people the immediate nationalization of the Suez Canal. There was popular jubilation, but the action was opposed by the British and French and, for security reasons, the Israelis. Troops were sent in, in what came to be known as the 'cowardly tripartite aggression': the Sinai was invaded, and attacks launched on Suez and Port Said. This was followed by a swift retreat, under pressure from America and the Soviet Union.

These events were to have major consequences for Alexandria, as all British, French and Jews were immediately expelled. Most went to Europe, although some of the Jews joined their coreligionists who had already left for Israel in 1948.

Four years after the king's departure, in 1956, Nasser ousted General Neguib. After his famous speech in Alexandria on 26 July when he announced the nationalization of the Suez Canal, he was driven in triumph through the crowd (above). Later, travelling on his special train, Nasser took almost a week to get back to Cairo: in the jubilation following his announcement, he was held up at every station by popular demonstrations.

The end of the foreign communities

The foreign exodus was hastened by the sequestration of assets, by land reform (from 1957 onwards), and by the nationalizations in the early 1960s that finally forced the Greeks and Syrian-Lebanese into exile, to Greece itself, to Canada and to Australia. One can imagine the pain these departures caused for families born in Alexandria, who had sometimes lived there for centuries and never known anywhere but Egypt. Half a century later, nostalgia is still strong, fostered in clubs from Montreal to Sydney where Alexandrians talk on into the night of their beloved city, never forgotten and sometimes magnified in recollection, which they were forced to quit, often with just a suitcase, leaving everything behind.

It was the end of the foreign communities, and the end of the cosmopolitan city in which Nasser, who spent part of his youth there, had never felt comfortable. The Egyptian government abandoned the age-old practice of spending the summer in Alexandria. Everything now focused on Cairo, and Alexandria reverted to its former sleepy state. The atmosphere of this somnolent city is vividly caught in Naguib Mahfouz's novel *Miramar*, where the sole foreigner is the woman running the pension

The first foreigners to be expelled as a result of the Suez affair were the French (below, arriving in Marseille) and the English (left, leaving Alexandria).

Many families left at a few hours' notice, carrying nothing more than a suitcase and leaving all their other possessions behind. The foreign communities are now no more than a memory. But the former Alexandrians still like to remember the past, and some have published memoirs that provide historians with valuable eyewitness accounts of life within the communities. Some also have real literary merit, and are poetic accounts of the exiles' attachment to their city, reflecting their intense concern to keep a part of their past history alive throughout the rest of their new lives.

where the hero lives. She alone dreams of the past, in a city that has become entirely Egyptian. Even the street names changed: Rue Fuad became el-Horraya (Liberty) Street, for instance, and Rue Chérif Pacha was renamed after Salah Salem, one of the officers in the *coup d'état*. (Alexandrians still today, however, go on calling the streets by their old names.)

European-style villas, and apartment blocks that might just as well be in Turin or Marseille, once proliferated in the eastern part of the city.

Now they are abandoned, and many of them have been pulled down. That was the fate of this apartment block with an octagonal tower in the Moharrem Bey area where Lawrence Durrell once lived, and which he described in letters to Henry Miller.

Economic disaster

Successive wars with Israel (1967, 1973) further worsened the economic situation. Building work had come to a stop, the housing stock was no longer maintained, apartment blocks were crumbling, lifts were permanently stuck between floors (rents had been frozen in 1963 at derisory levels, and leases were transferable), and imported products had disappeared from the shops. A state socialist economy was imposed, the streets were crawling with Russian advisers, rationing coupons made their appearance for basic supplies such as sugar and meat, not to mention coffee which had entirely vanished from the shelves; these goods could be bought only in state cooperatives, or at an inflated price on the black market. The inefficient and suspicious administration became more and more centralized, until all decisions were taken in Cairo, and Alexandrians had to go to the capital to obtain the most trivial sort of official certificate. The city was reduced to the status of Cairo's port. Popular discontent grew under the presidency of Anwar Sadat, and reached a climax in the hunger riots of January 1977: the Exchange – the building that symbolized capitalism, but that was also the setting

One of the great iconic images of the reconciliation of Egypt with the West is this scene of Richard Nixon, president of the United States, driven through the streets of Alexandria with President Sadat in 1974. The last war with Israel had taken place only a year earlier. Following his historic visit to Jerusalem in 1977, President Sadat embarked on an open door economic policy. Today the process of liberalizing the Egyptian economy continues, with the progressive privatization of the large state enterprises set up in the time of Nasser; but it is a difficult balancing act to perform without damage to the social fabric.

of Nasser's historic speech of 1956, was set alight; today the site is a parking lot.

A new surge of growth

Sadat's signing of the peace accords and his open door economic policy created the conditions for a limited resurgence of prosperity. Imports resumed, industries were set up on the southern shore of Lake Mariout, and Alexandria became Egypt's leading industrial area. The port was so busy that another had to be built at Dekheila, not far away to the west: more than 70 per cent of the country's exports pass through Alexandria.

In recent years, the municipal authority has encouraged businessmen to become financially involved in the city's revival. Facades have been repainted, new open spaces created, and the Corniche – now doubled in width – has recovered much of its past appeal. A few landmark projects have been launched, like the Bibliotheca Alexandrina, conceived of as rising like a phoenix from the ashes of the ancient Library. With a peacetime economy, construction has resumed; indeed, there has been a boom, as 19th-century buildings are rapidly replaced. Highrise apartment blocks, and office buildings in the city centre, are destroying the distinctive atmosphere that Alexandria retained for so long; and they have also had a disastrous effect on the city's ancient heritage. The depth at which archaeological remains were buried – up to 12 metres (40 feet) down – had hitherto ensured their survival. The 19th-century buildings with their shallow foundations simply sat on top of them. But the foundations of the new highrise developments extend deep down to the rocky substratum, passing through all the levels with traces of human habitation, and the situation is made worse still by the frequent provision of multi-storey parking areas under the buildings.

Alexandria still has two faces. While preserving what is left of the Turkish town and the vestiges of its cosmopolitan past (above), the city also looks resolutely to the future. The Bibliotheca Alexandrina (below) symbolizes the renaissance of the Mediterranean megalopolis in a modern Egypt.

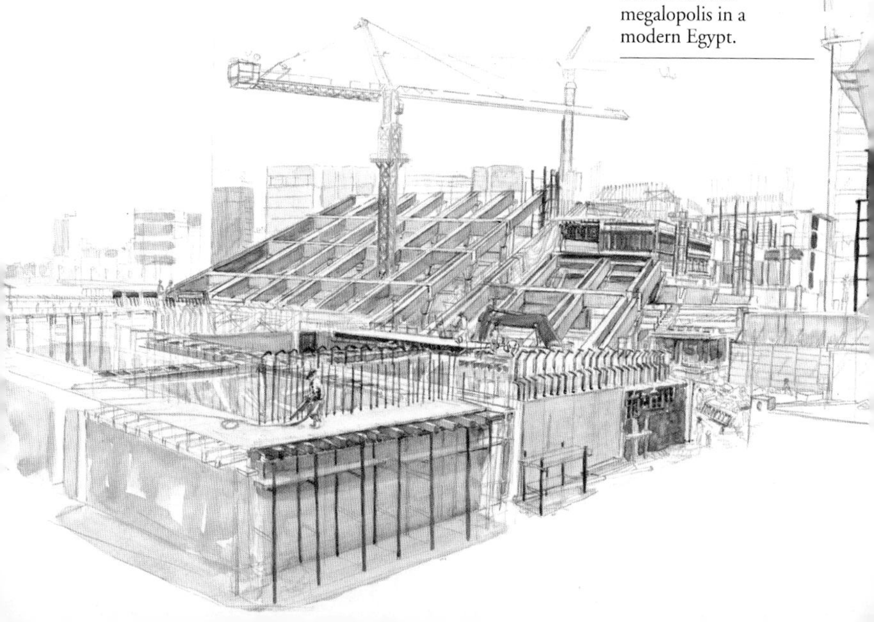

Alexandria has suffered from earthquakes, *tsunamis* and subsidence. The city has sunk several metres (more than 20 feet) over the centuries, and recent underwater excavations have revealed treasures hidden below the Mediterranean – remains of buildings, and also obelisks and a sphinx of the Pharaonic period from the sanctuary at Heliopolis, colossal statues of the Ptolemies, and more. In 1995 an immense figure of a Ptolemy depicted as a pharaoh was recovered, which once stood at the foot of the Pharos; it weighed with its base more than 70 tons, and was 13 m (42 feet) tall (above left and opposite, its raising and transport; above, the statue re-erected in Paris for the 1998 exhibition 'La Gloire d'Alexandrie'). Left: the Roman Odeon in the park of Kom el-Dick, the only archaeological site in the heart of the city.

Modernity versus heritage: an unequal struggle

The contest between rescue archaeologists and developers is unequally weighted, and the old Alexandrias are disappearing fast. Since 1960, the only archaeological remains preserved are those in the park of Kom el-Dick, which was set aside after the discovery of the only one to survive of Alexandria's four hundred theatres. Since then, everything has been destroyed, beyond hope of recovery. It seems no one can begin to imagine that the laying bare of Alexandria's heritage could actually enhance its tourist potential and one day become an economic asset. The construction of a metro line is awaited with some apprehension; with stations that are to be called Alexander's Tomb, the Library and the Necropolis, will it be the occasion for discovery or destruction?

Another recent phenomenon is the exploration of Alexandria's coastline, now being undertaken by a host of archaeological expeditions. The city has sunk 6–8 m (20–25 feet) since antiquity, and in the last few years Americans, Egyptians, French, Greeks and

Excavations in the city do not always have a happy outcome. In 1997, the construction of a motorway bridge in the western port area led to the chance discovery of part of the Necropolis, the large cemetery lying to the west of the city. The resumption of work in March 2000 meant the destruction of this whole archaeological complex. As the city is redeveloped there are many opportunities for rescue digs, but the developers are not always as interested as the archaeologists in preserving and enhancing the city's heritage.

Modern tower blocks (left) occupy the site of the ancient cemetery of Mustafa Kamel. On the site of the Diana Theatre, right in the heart of the city, a rescue dig (below) discovered Roman houses with extensive mosaics.

Overleaf: in the Latin cemeteries there stands a large antique alabaster tomb which archaeologists associate with the Tomb of Alexander the Great (see p. 18). Developers now have their eye on these extensive spaces, and it is to be hoped that rescue digs will be undertaken there.

Italians have been exploring the submerged edges of Alexandria, miraculously preserved because of settlement. Salvage archaeology within the city lacks support, but underwater exploration has media appeal and attracts a lot of interest.

Alexandria remains in the shadow of Cairo, but goes on searching for its own identity. A city throbbing with life, a wealthy hub of trade and industry, part of Egypt but facing out to the Mediterranean, a literary city and a city of memories, it still has a charm to which every visitor responds. Its rich history is set in magnificent surroundings, and its natural beauty has been shaped by human activity throughout millennia. There is the Corniche, which would not be out of place in Miami; the splendid neoclassical villas that can still be discovered between the skyscrapers; and the delicious surprise that awaits you when you round a street corner and happen upon the catacombs, where you can descend to the bowels of the city and discover the opulence of ancient Alexandria.

DOCUMENTS

Ancient sources

We have accounts of Alexander's city by the geographer Strabo (64/63 BC–AD 21) and the historian Plutarch (AD 46?–c. 120). The latter, in his 'Life of Alexander', recounts its legendary foundation. The former, who could draw both on written sources and on direct observation, gives us a unique description of the ancient city.

Plutarch

. . . Having conquered Egypt, Alexander determined to establish a great city there with a large Greek population, to which he would give his name. He was on the point of measuring and marking out a particular area, chosen on the advice of his architects, when during the night as he was sleeping he had a wonderful vision. He seemed to see a hoary old man with a venerable air approach and stand before him and recite these lines:

There lies an island in the churning sea
Hard against the Egyptian shore, called
Pharos.

When he arose he set out at once for Pharos. . . . Discovering it to be an exceptionally favourable site – for the island is in fact a spit of land not unlike a broad isthmus, running between a vast lagoon on the one side and a sound on the side of the sea, which culminates in a large harbour – he declared that Homer, among so many other admirable talents, also possessed that of architect, and he ordered a plan of the city to be marked out to correspond to the site. As they found no chalk to hand, they took barley meal to mark out on the black earth a curved circumference delineating an area that, with straight lines suspended inside it, would suggest the shape of a *chlamys* [cloak], tapering evenly from the bottom edge.

Life of Alexander

Strabo

The area occupied by the city is in the shape of a *chlamys*; the long sides of the *chlamys* are those bathed by the waters of the sea and of the lake, with a diameter of about 30 *stadia*, and the short sides are formed by the two isthmuses, each 7–9 *stadia* wide, that separate the sea on the one side and the lake on the other. Everywhere the city is crisscrossed with roads capable of being used by horsemen or drivers of carts; two of these are very broad, more than a plethron in width, and intersect at right angles. The city contains some splendid parks and the royal buildings, which occupy a quarter if not a third of the total area, for each of the kings, desirous in his turn of embellishing the public buildings with some new ornament, was no less desirous of adding, at his own expense, a further residence to those already in existence, so that now you can say of them, in the words of the poet: One is born out of another.

All these buildings form a continuous structure, [comprising] themselves, the port, and even those that lie beyond the port. The Mouseion too forms part of the royal buildings and comprises a *peripatos*, an exedra with seats, and a large building housing the commonroom where the scholars who are members of the Mouseion take their meals. This community of learned men enjoy common ownership of property, and there is a priest who is the head of the Mouseion, formerly appointed by the kings, now by Caesar. The place called Soma also forms part of the royal buildings. The precinct houses the royal sepulchres and that of Alexander. . . .

As you enter the Great Port, to your right you discover the island and tower of Pharos, to your left, the reefs and Cape Lochias, which has its own royal building. As you go further into the port, on your left you come to the royal buildings 'of the interior', which extend continuously on from that of Lochias, comprising wooded groves and numerous residences in a variety of styles. Below these buildings lies the man-made harbour, which is closed off, being the private property of the kings, as too is Antirhodos, the island across from the man-made harbour, which has a royal palace and little port of its own. It was so named as though it were a rival to Rhodes itself.

Above the man-made harbour are the theatre, then the Poseidion, curving sharply out from what is known as the Emporion, where a temple of Poseidon stands. Antony extended this projection into the middle of the harbour by means of a mole, at the end of which he built a royal residence given the name Timonion. . . . Then come the Kaisarion, the Emporion and the warehouses, and after them the arsenals, which extend all the way to the Heptastadion. . . .

Immediately after the Heptastadion comes the port of Eunostos and, beyond that, the man-made harbour called the Kibotos, which also has an arsenal. Further on, a canal that is navigable as far as Lake Mareotis debouches into the harbour. Beyond this canal, there is only a small part of the city left. Here the suburb of the Necropolis begins, where there are great numbers of gardens, tombs and reception places used for the mummification of the dead. On the side of the canal that is within the town, you see the Sarapion and other sacred precincts of great antiquity, now almost derelict. . . .

In a word, the city is full of public and sacred buildings, but the most handsome is the Gymnasium with its porticoes that extend for more than one *stadium*; in the middle are the tribune and the groves. Here too stands the Paneion, a man-made 'mound' in the shape of a pineapple which you would think was a rocky hill. A spiral path leads up to it. From the summit you can see the whole of the city, stretching out from its foot in all directions. The main road that runs the length of Alexandria starts at the Necropolis, passes the Gymnasium, and ends at the Canopic Gate. Then come the Hippodrome, so called, and the other [structures] that extend one after the other all the way to the Canopic Canal.

Geography, XVII

Cleopatra's Needles

In the early 19th century there was a thriving trade in Egyptian antiquities. With Mohammed Ali's blessing, Bernardino Drovetti and Henry Salt, the French and British consuls, amassed sizeable collections for the museums of Europe. Later, the Pasha gave the British one of the two obelisks erected by Augustus outside the Caesareum, and it arrived on the banks of the Thames in 1877. The second obelisk went to New York in 1879.

In front of the Caesareum (between present tram terminus and sea) stood Cleopatra's Needles of which one is now in the Central Park, New York, and the other on the Embankment, London. They had nothing to do with Cleopatra till after her death. They were cut in the granite quarries of Assouan for Thothmes III (B.C. 1500) and set up by him at Heliopolis near Cairo, before the temple of the Rising Sun. In B.C. 13 they were transferred here by the engineer Pontius. They rested not directly on their bases but each on four huge metal crabs, one of which has been recovered. Statues of Hermes or of Victory tipped them. In the Arab period, when all around decayed, they became the chief marvel of the city. One fell. They remained in situ until the 19th cent., when they were parted and took their last journey, the fallen one to England in 1877, the other to the United States two years later.

E. M. Forster
Alexandria, 1922

Transporting the English obelisk (left) proved no easy matter. The *Cleopatra*, a specially constructed cylindrical ship (opposite, middle and bottom left), was wrecked in the Bay of Biscay and had to be bought back from the captain of the salvage ship. The American obelisk encountered no such difficulties and was erected in Central Park before the eyes of an admiring crowd (opposite, above left and right and bottom right).

Travellers' tales

Alexandria has always attracted many visitors – Arab traders, pilgrims on their way to Mecca, Christians going to Jerusalem. They have left accounts that cover everything from their difficulties with customs to the habits of the local people, the vast scale of the walls, and the beauty of the cisterns. In the 19th and 20th centuries, the reactions express disappointment, fascination, and nostalgia.

We saw no other city . . . more beautiful or more full of life

The first scene we witnessed, on the day we arrived [1 April 1183], was the customs officers coming on board, in the name of the city's governor, to inspect the cargo.

All the Muslim passengers presented themselves, one after the other: their names, particulars and country of origin were recorded. Each was questioned as to the goods he was transporting and the money he had, to collect the *zakat* . . . One of our people, Ahmad ben Hassan, was made to disembark, and asked for news of the Maghreb and questioned about the ship's cargo. He was taken first of all under heavy escort to see the governor, then to the *cadi*, the customs officers, and a group of people from the governor's entourage; each of them questioned him and noted his words. Finally he was released. Then the Muslims were ordered to unload their baggage and any provisions they had left. On the quayside they were met by officials charged with escorting them to the customs post and bringing with them all their belongings. They were then called, one by one, and each man presented his baggage in the crush. It was all searched, both that with some value and that without, and all jumbled up together. Hands went inside belts looking for anything hidden. They were asked to swear they had nothing more than what had been found already. In the bustle, a lot of the baggage disappeared through sleight of hand or in the confusion. At last the Muslims were released, after this dreadfully humiliating and degrading experience . . .

We saw no other city where the streets are so vast or the buildings so tall, or that is more beautiful or more full of life. Its markets are very busy.

As for the construction of the city, it is astonishing that the underground structures are as extensive as those on the surface, and as beautiful and solidly built; this is because the waters of the Nile flow underground, beneath all the houses and streets. The wells thus adjoin

Opposite: The slave market, Alexandria.

one another and intercommunicate . . .

Among the virtues and claims to fame of this city, credit for which is due in reality to the sultan, are the madrasas and monasteries reserved for students and the devout who flock there from distant lands. There everyone finds accommodation, a master to teach him the branch of knowledge he wants to study, and a pension to provide for his needs. The sultan cares so much for these special foreigners that he has had baths installed which they use, and has founded a hospital where their sick are cared for and where doctors treat them, who have at their command assistants to fill the medical prescriptions and to see to regimes ordered by the doctors for the benefit of the sick. The sultan has also appointed people charged with visiting patients who choose not to go to hospital, especially foreigners, and with presenting their cases to the doctors so they can superintend their treatment . . .

It is curious that in this city the people have the same occupations night and day. This is also the city with the most mosques, to the point that any estimate is approximate only: some exaggerate their numbers, others underestimate them; the former arrive at twelve thousand, the latter calculate rather less, something like eight thousand. They are indeed very numerous, four or five on the same spot, and sometimes one comprises several.

Ibn Jubayr
Travels, early 12th century

All the eye can see is sand, water, and the everlasting Pompey's Pillar

I had been enchanted with Egypt, but Alexandria struck me as the saddest and most desolate place on earth. . . .

The ruins of the new Alexandria all jumbled up with the ruins of the ancient city; an Arab galloping through the

rubble on a donkey; a few thin dogs devouring camels' carcasses on the shore; the flags of the European consuls flying over their residences, displaying enemy colours amid the tombs: this is what you saw.

Sometimes I would go out riding with M. Drovetti, and we would go round the old town or the Necropolis or out into the desert. The arid sand was sparsely covered with saltwort; jackals took off as we approached; the shrill intrusive voice of a sort of cicada made itself heard, bringing painfully to mind the peasant hearth and home, in this wilderness where no rustic plume of smoke guides you to the Arab's tent. The place is the more dreary because the English flooded the vast basin that served Alexandria as its garden: all the eye can see is sand, water, and the everlasting Pompey's Pillar.

On the flat roof of his house M. Drovetti had constructed a tent-shaped aviary in which he reared various species of quail and partridge. We spent hours walking round this aviary talking about France. The conclusion of all our conversations was that we should at once start looking for some little retreat in our native land to which we could withdraw as the culmination of our hopes and dreams. One day, after a long discussion about peaceful retirement, I turned towards the sea and pointed out to my host the wind-buffeted vessel on which I was soon to embark. When all is said and done, it is not that the desire for retirement is unnatural in a man; but what seems to us the most modest goal is not always the easiest to attain, and the cottage often remains as distant a prospect as the palace.

René de Chateaubriand
Journey from Paris to Jerusalem, 1811

All that is destroyed, razed to the ground, unrecognizable

Egypt is one vast tomb; that was the impression it made on me as I landed on the beach at Alexandria, which displays a prospect of ruins and low mounds, a few scattered tombs on an ashen soil.

Shades draped in bluish shrouds move among the debris. I went and saw Pompey's Pillar and Cleopatra's Baths. The walk along the Mahmoudiya with its evergreen palms provides the only reminder of living nature . . .

I will spare you the details of a big and very European square made up of the palaces of the consuls and the houses of the bankers, the Byzantine churches in ruins, and the modern structures built by the Pasha of Egypt, with gardens resembling hothouses. I would have preferred some memorials of Greek antiquity, but all that is destroyed, razed to the ground, unrecognizable.

Gérard de Nerval
Travels in the East, 1851

I gulped down colour, like a donkey gorging itself on oats

When we were two hours out from the Egyptian shore, I went up into the bow with the chief helmsman and I made out the harem of Abbas Pasha, like a black dome against the blue of the sea. The sunlight was beating down on it. I could make out the Orient through it, or, rather, in a great haze of silver light dissolving over the sea. Soon the shoreline took shape, and the first thing we saw on land was two camels being led by a camel driver, and all along the quayside some fine Arab fellows fishing with lines in the most peaceable manner in the world. When we disembarked there was the most deafening racket in the world, with negroes, negresses, camels, turbans, blows raining down left and right, accompanied by earsplitting guttural cries. I gulped down colour, like a donkey gorging itself on oats. – The stick plays a big role here, anything wearing a clean robe thrashes anything wearing a dirty robe, or indeed no robe at all: when I say robe, breeches is what I really mean to say. You see a number of gentlemen lounging about the streets with nothing but a shirt and a long pipe. Apart from those of the lowest class, all the women are veiled, with ornaments over their noses that dangle and swing like a horse's harness ornament. But while you do not see their faces, you certainly do see their bosoms. – When modesty moves from one country to another it also changes position, like a bored traveller who sometimes sits up top, sometimes in the boot. One curious thing here is the respect, indeed fear, they have for the Frank. We saw groups of ten or twelve Arabs, occupying the whole width of the street, move out of the way to let us pass. Alexandria I may add is almost European, there are so many Europeans here. There are thirty or so of us at table at our hotel alone. Everywhere is full of English, Italians, etc.

Gustave Flaubert
Letter to his mother, 1849

City of contrasts. Full of comings and goings, a colonial air . . .

Half past seven in the morning, clear skies above, sun shining, and on the southeastern horizon we see something above the sea. Trees, we're told. Palms of course. The blobs get closer, become clearer, a low coastline comes into view.

Backgammon players

One hour later, the whole of the Libyan coast and all of Alexandria are visible . . .

Alexandria. City of contrasts. Full of comings and goings, a colonial air, clearly a place where foreigners live.

Very handsome bits of wall, very handsome indeed. Outer boulevards. First truly Egyptian physiognomy. It really hits you when you see your first fellah, and the first convoy of dromedaries with which I renew my acquaintance makes my heart beat faster. We emerge from the Frankish quarter and visit the Arab quarters: really quite extraordinary; but once you have seen Cairo, nothing by comparison.

Argument in the fruit market. A woman, a real snarling lioness: nothing could be wilder, more raucous or more frightening. Fearsome jaw, eyes flashing, formidable gestures, and the same exasperation and the same imprecations over and over again for a whole quarter of an hour, with not a hint of tiredness and with a continually redoubled force you would not believe. Her companion, long, thin, silent, strictly veiled, wearing dark crepe, black headdress covered all over with silver chains wrapped round her pretty head: was she pretty? Crooking her bare left arm with its silver ornaments, her hand with its orangey palm, without uttering a word, without moving, she propped her chin on her hand, waiting for her irate friend to vent her anger.

Potbellied children eaten by flies.

Eugène Fromentin
Journey to Egypt, 1869

It is only the merchants of Alexandria, buying cotton

'Oh, Heaven help us! What is that dreadful noise? Run, run! Has somebody been killed?'

'Do not distress yourself, kind-hearted sir. It is only the merchants of Alexandria, buying cotton.'

'But they are murdering one another surely.'

'Not so. They merely gesticulate.'

'Does any place exist whence one could view their gestures in safety?'

'There is such a place.'

'I shall come to no bodily harm there?'

'None, none.'

'Then conduct me, pray.'

And mounting to an upper chamber we looked down into a stupendous Hall.

It is usual to compare such visions to Dante's Inferno, but this really did resemble it, because it was marked out into the concentric circles of which the Florentine speaks. Divided from each other by ornamental balustrades, they increased in torment as they decreased in size, so that the inmost ring was congested beyond redemption with perspiring souls. They shouted and waved and spat at each other across the central basin which was empty but for a permanent official who sat there, fixed in ice. Now and then he rang a little bell, and now and then another official, who dwelt upon a ladder far away, climbed and wrote upon a board with chalk. The merchants hit their heads and howled. A terrible calm ensued. Something worse was coming. While it gathered we spoke.

'Oh, name this place!'

'It is none other than the Bourse. Cotton is sold at this end, Stocks and Shares at that.'

E. M. Forster,
Pharos and Pharillon, 1923

Yes, it was dances every day . . . People had great taste in Alexandria

In the glass cases at the Yacht Club there are still heaps of old regatta cups; up on the roof, the wind turns the pages of a complete bound collection of *The Rudder*, a venerable British sailing magazine, warped by the weather. In the dining room, the maître d'hôtel, whose bow tie has nourished entire squadrons of moth, is very sorry he can no longer serve you wine, as the sea casts quivering reflections on the ceiling. 'Yes,' an old Alexandrian woman recalls without bitterness, 'it was dances every day . . . The evenings when Madame Salvago and all the ladies from the big cotton families went to the Mohammed Ali Theatre, the boxes used to glitter with jewels . . .' Through the windows you can see the perfect curve of the Eastern Port extending before you, from the fort built on the foundations of the ancient lighthouse, on towards Chatby-les-Bains, Glymenopoulos, Stanley Beach, San Stefano, the beaches with their old European names, now dominated by an unbroken stretch of crumbling concrete wall. 'When you went down the Rue Chérif,' the old lady reminisces, 'from one end of it to the other you breathed Chanel No 5. People had great taste in Alexandria . . . ' She is shortly to take the inspector of ruins to the Moharrem Bey quarter, behind the Cairo station. 'Old gardens reflected in the eyes', big dusty villas slumbering among the building sites. Only the extravagant grey, ochre and pink palace in Rue Badawi that Durrell used as the model for Nessim's house has held out against decay: it is occupied by the Chinese consulate. 'An Italian architect used to live there. He was so jealous he kept his wife a prisoner. The poor thing . . . We used to play at the Sporting Club together.' A handsome chair with a jute sack for a cushion in the porter's lodge must have come from Justine's salon. The old lady searches for the Ambron house, where Durrell once lived. Is it this one, with a turret, and a caved-in roof? Or is it that one, with the porphyry columns? 'I need to find someone old. The young don't know anything about those days anymore.' A facade with closed shutters elicits a little laugh: 'The woman who owned this house used to buy the attentions of the best-looking boy in town with paintings by Dufy . . . One night, one Dufy . . .' A rusty gate leads in to the long gardens of the Levi house. The trees, the bowers have taken on a dull golden hue . . . Between some fallen capitals, an old man is planting out lettuces, oblivious to the hunters of memories. The house is tall and still; it seems to be a place where life has slowed down, where it is lived discreetly, clandestinely almost, and silently, right in the middle of the tumult of Alexandria. For a second the face of a squatter appears behind a raised curtain. The old lady remembers coming here for a costume ball in 1900. 'I had purple boots. Inside, it was a dream . . . What furniture! What porcelain!' The music pavilion has been pulled down, a curiosity that has had its day. On the path outside, a duck waddles past a cobbler's booth made of cardboard.

Olivier Rolin
Sept villes, 1988

I'm interested in Alexandria

I had been in Alexandria for twenty-four hours (already aware that I would remain attached to my first landmarks, my first encounters, like a donkey tied to its stake, and that every time I came back I would again seek out the freshness of those first experiences), when a man with jogging pants and rolls of fat addressed me:

'Are you visiting Egypt?'

'No, just Alexandria.'

He started as if a wasp had stung him, then turned his big compassionate eyes on me. He was a man of about thirty. The beginnings of a beard darkened his olive cheeks.

'Why not Aswan or Cairo? It's no more expensive.'

'It's Alexandria that interests me.'

There was no longer any trace of pity or friendliness in his expression. I very quickly got the impression that I disgusted him, and he would have liked to crush me under the heels of his big Nikes, simply because of what I had just said: 'I'm interested in Alexandria.'

He burst out laughing:

'You, very funny man, here there's nothing to see, you hear me, nothing to see.'

Daniel Rondeau
Alexandrie, 1997

Alexandria in literature

Of the Greek, Italian, English, French and of course Egyptian authors who found inspiration in Alexandria, some were born in the city, while others only lived there for a few years. Novels, novellas, poems and songs, all genres are represented, and all languages. Among them are masterpieces of world literature, by such illustrious writers as Cavafy, Durrell, Mahfouz and, more recently, Edwar Al-Kharrat.

Constantine Cavafy (1863–1933)

Tomb of Iasis

I, Iasis, lie here – famous for my good
looks
in this great city.
The wise admired me, so did common,
superficial people.
I took equal pleasure in both.

But from being considered so often a
Narcissus and Hermes,
excess wore me out, killed me. Traveller,
if you're an Alexandrian, you won't
blame me.
You know the pace of our life – its
fever, its absolute devotion to pleasure.

The City

You said: 'I'll go to another country, go
to another shore,
find another city better than this one.
Whatever I try to do is fated to turn out
wrong
and my heart – like something dead –
lies buried.
How long can I let my mind moulder in
this place?
Wherever I turn, wherever I look,
I see the black ruins of my life, here,
where I've spent so many years, wasted
them, destroyed them totally.'

You won't find a new country, won't find
another shore.
The city will always pursue you.
You'll walk the same streets, grow old
in the same neighbourhoods, turn grey
in these same houses.
You'll always end up in this city. Don't
hope for things elsewhere:
there's no ship for you, there's no road.
Now that you've wasted your life here,
in this small corner,
you've destroyed it everywhere in the
world.

The God Abandons Antony

At midnight, when suddenly you hear
an invisible procession going by
with exquisite music, voices,
don't mourn your luck that's failing now,
work gone wrong, your plans
all proving deceptive – don't mourn
them uselessly:
as one long prepared, and full of courage,

say goodbye to her, to Alexandria who is leaving.
Above all, don't fool yourself, don't say
it was a dream, your ears deceived you:
don't degrade yourself with empty hopes like these.
As one long prepared, and full of courage,
as is right for you who were given this kind of city,
go firmly to the window
and listen with deep emotion,
but not with the whining, the pleas of a coward;
listen – your final pleasure – to the voices,
to the exquisite music of that strange procession,
and say goodbye to her, to the Alexandria you are losing.

Days of 1909, '10, and '11

He was the son of a misused, poverty-stricken sailor
(from an island in the Aegean Sea).
He worked for an ironmonger: his clothes shabby,
his workshoes miserably torn,
his hands filthy with rust and oil.

In the evenings, after the shop closed,
if there was something he longed for especially,
a more or less expensive tie,
a tie for Sunday,
or if he saw and coveted
a beautiful blue shirt in some store window,
he'd sell his body for a half-crown or two.

I ask myself if the great Alexandria
of ancient times could boast of a boy
more exquisite, more perfect –
thoroughly neglected though he was:
that is, we don't have a statue or painting of him;
thrust into that poor ironmonger's shop,
overworked, harassed, given to cheap debauchery,
he was soon used up.

Collected Poems
Translated by Edmund Keeley
and Philip Sherrard, 1978

Giuseppe Ungaretti (1888–1970)

Levant *

The line of smoke
dies out upon
the distant ring of the sky

Clatter of heels clapping of hands
and the clarinet's shrill flourishes
and the sky is ashen
trembles gentle uneasy
like a dove

In the stern Syrian emigrants are dancing

In the bow a young man is alone

On Saturday evenings at this time
Jews
in those parts
carry away
their dead
through the shell's spiralling
uncertainties
of alleyways
of lights

Churning of water
like the racket from the stern
that I hear within the shadow
of
sleep

*Ungaretti is leaving Alexandria, his birthplace, on his way to France; 'in those parts' refers to Alexandria.

Silence

Mariano, 27 June 1916
I know a city
that every day fills to the brim with
sunlight
and in that instant everything is
enchanted

I left one evening

In my heart the rasp of the cicadas went
on

From the white
painted vessel
I saw
my city disappear
leaving
an embrace of lights
for a while
in the troubled air
hanging

Selected Poems, 1971
Translated by Patrick Creagh

Stratis Tsirkas (1911–80)

While he talked, he opened the French window and led me out on the balcony. The sea was suddenly revealed to us, calm and shining; it took my breath away. Huge clouds floated in the sky, filled with light. Across the sea, on the ancient island of Pharos, the mute, heavy bulk of the Kait Bey Fort lay reflected in the still waters, like a cheap water color intended for tourists. We leaned over the balcony to take in the Eastern Harbor, following the waterfront with our gaze up to the point where the street turns upward for Ramleh. I had the impression of standing on the tiers of a great stadium or arena. Down below, to the right, on Cape Silsileh (Strabo refers to it as Cape Lochias, Paraschos informed me), among the camouflaged cannons, the projectors, the radars – that's where the dressing rooms would be, I thought, continuing the arena fantasy: a small side door opens and the bull charges through . . . Then again the soft curves of the coast ensnared my eyes, those serpentine, feminine lines, those hesitations, coves and bays opening up suddenly, revealing fine yellow crescents of sand. Paraschos pointed with his finger, explaining the geography to me. As landmarks, he chose an apartment building with a flashing inscription near Cape Silsileh and, farther to the east, the Greek Hospital on Aboukir Avenue. Between these two landmarks lay the Chatby cemeteries. That was where Antoinos's bones were slowly wasting away, giving back to the earth the little substance he had borrowed from it in his lifetime. He had taken nothing away with him and he had left nothing behind – nothing but memories.

'Just think,' said Paraschos, 'if Antoinos were to rise from his grave, with his big stick, his hobnailed boots, his heavy walk . . . how his soul would rejoice at the sight of Alexandria today, exactly the way he liked to dream of it. He'd twirl his mustache and rub the back of his wrinkled neck, pleased as Punch. "You nitwits," he used to say to us, "try and get this into your thick skulls, who do you think we are? We're only guests in this city. We came here, we settled down nice and comfortable, we raised sons and grandsons. Fine. But our host was fast asleep all the while – isn't that so? Well, let's wake him up, I say. Let's ask his permission, and let him say we're welcome, so that everything between us is put straight and we may all be at peace. Because if he does wake up one day – and he will, mark my words – and finds us sitting pretty in his land, he'd give us one mighty kick in the arse and fling us straight into the sea. And he'll be quite right too – we'll just have to swallow it without a word. Don't listen to all those clever guys who sit in their offices and wear hard collars. They are Westerners, Europeans. They speak like Europeans, they go around with Europeans, their minds work the European way. All they think about is dough, how to get more and more of it and then spend it on smart trips to Europe. This isn't their country; they have no feeling for it. This land, you see, is a great juicy female, full of eggs, like those grey mullet we fish with a cast net when they come downstream in August. But if you want her to grow big and spawn – well it takes guts, it takes hard work, you've got to drive yourself to the limit, panting and gasping atop of her. It's too big a job for us, her guests, we're not up to it. What she wants is her master. So hand her over to these people here; she belongs to them, and you'll see the results. The whole coast will fill up with little swarming men, who'll build tall buildings and factories, schools and theaters, who'll open up new roads, big streets and little streets, and start coffee shops where you can sip your aniseed drink and have a chat with God. They'll plant parks too. All this yellow stretch of land will be dotted with red fezzes and black haiks, the way poppies fill the desert in springtime."'

Drifting Cities, 1974
Translated by Kay Cicellis

Lawrence Durrell (1912–90)

Hereabouts it would be a hundred to one that he would ever be recognized – for few Europeans ever came into this part of the city. The quarter lying beyond the red lantern belt, populated by the small traders, money-lenders, coffee-speculators, ships' chandlers, smugglers; here in the open street one had the illusion of time spread out flat – so to speak – like the skin of an ox; the map of time which one could read from one end to the other, filling it in with known points of reference. This world of Moslem time stretched back to Othello and beyond – cafés sweet with the trilling of singing birds whose cages were full of mirrors to give them the illusion of company. The love-songs of birds to companions they imagined – which were only reflections of themselves! How heartbreakingly they sang, these illustrations of human love! Here too in the ghastly breath of the naphtha flares the old eunuchs sat at *trictrac*, smoking the long nargilehs which at every drawn breath loosed a musical bubble of sound like a dove's sob; the walls of the old cafés were stained by the sweat from the tarbushes hanging on the pegs; their collections of coloured nargilehs were laid up in rows in a long rack, like muskets, for which each tobacco-drinker brought his cherished personal holder. . . . He was perfectly at his ease, now; he had come to terms with his unfamiliar state of befuddlement and no longer felt that he was drunk; it was simply that he had become inflated now by a sense of tremendous dignity and self-importance which gave him a grandiose deliberation of movement. He walked slowly, like a pregnant woman nearing term, drinking in the sights and sounds.

Mountolive, 1958

Walking about the streets of the summer capital once more, walking by spring sunlight, and a cloudless skirmishing blue sea – half-asleep and half-awake – I felt like the Adam of the mediaeval legends: the world-compounded body of a man whose flesh was soil, whose bones were stones, whose blood water, whose hair was grass, whose eyesight sunlight, whose breath was wind, and whose thoughts were clouds. And weightless now, as if after some long wasting illness, I found myself turned adrift again to float upon the shallows of Mareotis with its old tide-marks of appetites and desires refunded into the history of the place: an ancient city with all its cruelties intact, pitched upon a desert and a lake. Walking down with remembered grooves of streets which extended on every side, radiating out like the arms of a starfish from the axis of its founder's tomb. Footfalls echoing in the memory, forgotten scenes and conversations springing up at me from the walls, the café tables, the shuttered rooms with cracked and peeling ceilings. Alexandria, princess and whore. The royal city and the *anus mundi*. She would never change so long as the races continued to seethe here like must in a vat; so long as the streets and squares still gushed and spouted with the fermentation of these diverse passions and spites, rages and sudden calms. A fecund desert of human loves littered with the whitening bones of its exiles. Tall palms and minarets marrying in the sky. A hive of white mansions flanking those narrow and abandoned streets of mud which were racked all night by Arab music and the cries of girls who so easily disposed of their body's wearisome baggage (which galled them) and offered to the night the passionate kisses which money could not disflavour. . . .

A whole new geography of Alexandria was born through Clea, reviving old meanings, renewing ambiences half forgotten, laying down like a rich wash of colour a new history, a new biography to replace the old one. Memory of old cafés along the seafront by bronze moonlight, their striped awnings a-flutter with the midnight sea-breeze. To sit and dine late, until the glasses before one had brimmed with moonlight. In the shadow of a minaret, or on some strip of sand lit by the twinkle of a paraffin lamp. Or gathering the masses of shallow spring blossom on the Cape of Figs – brilliant cyclamen, brilliant anemone. Or standing together in the tombs of Kom El Shugafa inhaling the damp exhalations of the darkness which welled out of those strange subterranean resting-places of Alexandrians long dead; tombs carved out of the black chocolate soil, one upon the other, like bunks in a ship. Airless, mouldy and yet somehow piercingly cold.

Clea, 1960

At Alexandria

Sometime we shall all come together
And it will be time to put a stop
To this little rubbing together of
minimal words,
To let the Word Prime repose in its
mode
As yolk in its fort of albumen reposes,
Contented by the circular propriety
Of its hammock in the formal breathing
egg.

Much as in sculpture the idea
Must not of its own anecdotal grossness
Sink through the armature of the
material,
The model of its earthly clothing:
But be a plumbline to its weight
in space . . .
The whole resting upon the ideogram
As on a knifeblade, never really cutting,
Yet always sharp, like this very metaphor
For perpetual and *useless* suffering
exposed by conscience in the very act
of writing.

Collected Poems 1931–1974, 1985

Naguib Mahfouz (born 1912)

The massive old building confronts me once again. How could I fail to recognize it? I have always known it. And yet it regards me as if we had shared no past. Walls paintless from the damp, it commands and dominates the tongue of land, planted with palms and leafy acacias, that protrudes out into the Mediterranean to a point where in season you can hear shotguns cracking incessantly.

My poor stooped body cannot stand up to the potent young breeze out here. Not anymore.

Mariana, my dear Mariana, let us hope you're still where we could always find you. You must be. There's not much time left; the world is changing fast and my weak eyes under their thinning white brows can no longer comprehend what they see.

Alexandria, I am here.

On the fourth floor I ring the bell of the flat. The little judas opens, showing Mariana's face. Much changed, my dear! It's dark on the landing; she does not recognize me. Her white face and golden hair gleam in the light from a window open somewhere behind her.

'Pension Miramar?'

'Yes, monsieur?'

'Do you have any vacant rooms?'

The door opens. The bronze statue of the Madonna receives me. In the air of the place is a kind of fragrance that has haunted me.

We stand looking at each other. She is tall and slim, with her golden hair, and seems to be in good health, though her shoulders are a little bowed and the hair is obviously dyed. Veins show through the skin of her hands and forearms; there are telltale wrinkles at the corners of her mouth. You must be sixty-five at least, my dear, But there is still something of the old glamour left. I wonder if you'll remember me.

She looks me over. At first she examines me; then the blue eyes blink. Ah, you remember! And my self comes back to me.

'Oh! It's you.'

'Madame.'

We shake hands warmly – 'Goodness me! Amer Bey! Monsieur Amer!' – and she laughs out loud with emotion (*the long feminine laugh of the fishwives of Anfushi!*) . . .

Miramar, 1993
Translated by Fatma Moussa Mahmoud

Edwar Al-Kharrat (born 1926)

The sky above me had become terrible, enormously high, harbouring death in its bowels, crushing, heavy, final, inevitable. The all-encompassing brilliance of the moon was cruel. The searchlight beams made long moving swords of cutting light, coming both from the edges of the city and from the centre; they turned in the clear silken blueness, crossing and parting, veering away and swinging together again so that the ends met for an instant and fixed upon a small shining dot; branching out once more to probe the inscrutable belly of the sky, scouring it again for the ducking, weaving spot of treachery. The burst of ack-ack fire, thin and piercing and continuous, rattled ceaselessly, exploding in great metallic red flowers whose sparks scattered suddenly and as suddenly were extinguished. The roar of the aeroplane engines was far and high, but audible between the bursts of fire from the anti-aircraft guns, in the silence which made the city seem even more fragile, even more laid bare, from el-Anfushi to el-Mandara and el-Montaza, from el-Rand and el-Ban and el-Nakhil in Gheit el-Enab to el-Labban and Ra's el-Tin and Anastasi; from Glymonopoulo and Zizinia to Stanley and el-Nuzha and el-Wardyan; from Hagar el-Nawatiya to Kom el-Nadura, from Sidi Gabir and Sidi Bishr and Bacos to Samuha and el-Maks; from the Cairo railway station and el-Rassafa to Mustafa Pasha, and back again to 'Ezbet el-Sayadin.

All the treasures of Alexandria lay prostrate and naked, veiled only by the network of beams which stabbed the sky.

During that night a bomb was dropped from the Italian plane above the tomb of Sidi Abu'l Dardar; but it never landed on the tomb.

Eye-witnesses said that while the bomb's fat body plunged spinning through the air, its pointed end aimed downwards, gleaming evilly in the moonlight, the green dome of the tomb, which was in the middle of a leafy vine-trellis surrounded by a thin iron railing, cracked open and then at once sealed up again, and there rose from it the Holy Presence of the Saint.

He was one of the Righteous! He redeemed his people, all the sons of his God-preserved white city! His yellow Moroccan *burnous* flapped open in the breeze like two wings, and his face was like the rising full moon, eclipsing the full disc in the sky. His aura dazzled the sight, and the smell of musk and ambergris wafted out from the sealed tomb. He spread out his wide, shining arms to receive the dreadful bomb, hurtling down like a thunderbolt into his embrace, and, lo! it became cold, and safe. The Saint sped away in the twinkling of an eye or faster, and took the bomb at once to the high green deserted hill at el-Shallalat, and laid it on its side on the ground. Its evil and harm had been taken away, and it lay there among the twisted trees, cold, iron and dead, with no power nor might.

The people found it early the next morning. They flocked to it in their thousands together; they took it to pieces without it doing them any harm, without difficulty. Everybody took away a piece of scrap metal as a blessing – and a souvenir.

When the soldiers came up from the garrison to put a cordon around the area, there was nothing left of the terrible bomb except some small brittle pieces of tin, and a pile, crumbled and cold, of gunpowder that looked like ground red pepper.

City of Saffron, 1989
Translated by Frances Liardet

Robert Solé (born 1946)

Lying face down on the damp sand, a little dizzy from the midday sun, Lola was daydreaming. Dying waves came and lapped her feet, her calves, sometimes right up to her thighs, making her whole body quiver with pleasure. She was lovely enough to eat and beginning to know it. . . .

They all knew one other on this beach at Glymenopoulo that had been colonized by the Syrians, while the Jews occupied nearby Stanley Beach. You felt at home, among your own. To the point that you would loudly express your surprise if a Coptic or Muslim family had the poor taste to move in and plant their sun umbrella.

Lola adored these long summer holidays in Alexandria. For weeks in advance, she had dreamed of arriving in Sidi Gaber station and the great big black taxi, belching smoke, that would take them to the villa. In her room she rediscovered her old toys waiting quietly in their places. She caressed them, sniffed them, sometimes put her tongue on them to make sure they still tasted of salt. Then, with Viviane close behind, she ran to the next-door houses to meet up with cousins and friends. . . .

The first Sunday in August, the children joined in the traditional visit to the Touta cousins in Sidi Bishr. This was the Alexandrian branch of the family – 'the crazy branch', Georges said, making it quite clear the problem lay on his brother-in-law Edmond's side of the family.

There were eleven brothers and sisters, to all of whom their parents had given pharaonic names. Sesostris, the oldest, promoted to Bey at under forty, had taken it into his head to live in a steamship. This senior official had built himself a house in the form of a ship, 30 metres [100 feet] or so long, facing out to sea. It had everything, deck and bridge, not to mention ladders, gangways and hatches.

Sesostris Bey, wearing an admiral's hat, received visitors on the poop deck. His sisters Isis and Nephthys handed round cakes and drinks for the children. They were in ecstasies because they were allowed to sweep the sea with the master of the house's big binoculars.

All the cabmen in Ramleh knew the address. You just had to say: We want the home of Sesostris Bey.

The vehicle passed through quiet streets edged with tamarisk, behind which slumbered vast houses with *mashrabiyya*, swamped in vegetation. The cab's bell pierced the silence, sometimes in response to another cabby's complaint. The children shut their eyes the better to smell the scent of the seaweed. Alexandria in those days smelt of sea and jasmine.

Le Tarbouche, 1992

The Latin cemeteries of Alexandria

Like the cemeteries of antiquity and their Muslim successors, the 19th-century Latin cemeteries were built outside the city walls. Bisected by Rue Anubis, and extending over more than 18 hectares (45 acres), these green open spaces are now threatened by the expansion of the 21st-century city. Here lie Jews, freethinkers, Copts, Armenians, Anglicans, Greeks and Catholics.

The western cemeteries, north to south

If you credit the inscriptions – mostly in Italian – the Jewish cemetery is the repository of the finest moral and intellectual values in all Alexandria. The 'sublime mothers' and 'tender and affectionate fathers' are beyond counting, and even the visitor with the most sceptical view of human nature cannot fail to be impressed by '*X, uomo laborioso e onesto, marito e padre affettuosissimo*', 'X, example of the noble vertues of faith, goodness and resignation', '*X, persona distinta e filantropica*', and so on.

The Old British Protestant Cemetery, consecrated by the Bishop of Jerusalem on 28 April 1916, is somewhat neglected; the small number of graves suggests that bodies were repatriated. The empty spaces between the graves are filled with vegetation so dense you would think you were in a botanical garden. . . .

The 'Cemetery of the Greek Community of Alexandria' is, when it comes to monuments, and I use the word advisedly, the most opulent of them all: when you arrive by car from the airport you see what looks like the top of a *tholos* poking above the perimeter wall; this proves to be a fairly faithful copy of the Choragic monument of Lysicrates in Athens, in this case retaining its bronze tripod. It is the last resting place of Emmanuel Kasadagli. . . . There is no end to these monuments (colonnades, miniature temples, a Greek village church, a host of angels), the chief merit of which is to emphasize the simplicity of the gravestone beneath which Constantine Cavafy is laid to rest, near his compatriots but apart from them. No date of birth, just when he died: Alexandria, 28 April 1933. And under his name, the single word: 'poet'.

The 'Cemetery of the Catholic Greek Community' is as small as it is plain. Oddly and unexpectedly, it is full of patronymics with echoes of antiquity. The attributes of 'Faraone' or 'Hermes' were indeed much respected in the second Alexandria, but 'Sotiriou' is interesting: the Pharos was dedicated by Sostratus of Cnidos to the 'saviour gods'.

On emerging from here, you need to have the gates of the vast 'cimitero latino di Terra Santa' opened for you by its caretaker, an Italian Franciscan monk (in jeans and short-sleeved shirt) who has been here, quite comfortably, for twenty years, rears his dogs here and assures you with a smile that he would die of grief if he had to leave his beloved cimitero . . .

To the right of the entrance, an ancient sarcophagus holds the remains of Joseph Botti, the famous archaeologist and first curator of the city's Greco-Roman museum. Farther on, under obelisks, cherubim and pyramids, lie Alexandrians whose names make up a sort of recitation that even Durrell, who must have known these people, would not have dared use in his books because no one would have believed it: Brillet, Dentamaro, Enriquez, Sidarouss, Tron, Gallo, Grill Sivitz, Imperadore, Trad, Buccianti, Jacopech, Recoulin, Degiardé, Gebeyli, Ablitt, Darmenia Macdonald . . .

The eastern cemeteries, north to south

The Armenian cemetery has a church and chapel in the purest style of the distant homeland . . . Appropriately enough, almost all the epitaphs are written in Armenian script, but there are exceptions. One is that of the Vartanian family, which has a Greek portico in a state of (artificial) ruin. Another is this unusual epitaph: 'Here lies Hovsep. A. Tcherkesian, born in Amassia, (Turkey). Year 1839. Moved to Alexandria in 1874, where he founded the first business dealing in string. Died a bachelor in Alexandria on 26 December 1898.' A marble ball of string decorates the tomb.

Alongside is the 'Egyptian Greek Orthodox Cemetery', distinguished from the rest only by its mean proportions and drab appearance.

The adjacent 'War Memorial Cemetery 1914–1918' is exclusively military. Should we exclude it from our exploration of Alexandria's past, on the grounds that all it tells us about is war? Alas, war is a part of that past, embracing the Second World War as well as the First.

The 'British Protestant Cemetery' that comes next is almost empty, and the many tombs lying open again suggest repatriation, although in this case on a massive scale.

The 'Orthodox Egyptian Cemetery', which inscriptions in Arabic script announce to be Coptic, has no discernible character at all.

Next and last is the Jewish Cemetery. With the exception of the mausoleum of the Habib de Toledano family, it does not differ significantly from the preceding example: same names, similar epitaphs.

Alexandria has several remembered pasts. There is the one handed down to us by Greek and Roman historians, supplemented latterly by excavation and scholarship; and there is the one handed down to us by poets and novelists, Cavafy, Tsirkas, Forster, Durrell – but that remembered past relates, perhaps, to a different Alexandria, either truer or falser than nature, an Alexandria of dreams. It is in its cemeteries, guarded by yellow Anubises that are on the whole benevolent, that the real history of the second Alexandria is to be sought.

Lucien Basch
'Les Jardins des morts'
in 'Alexandrie en Egypte',
Méditerranéennes, 8/9,
Autumn 1996

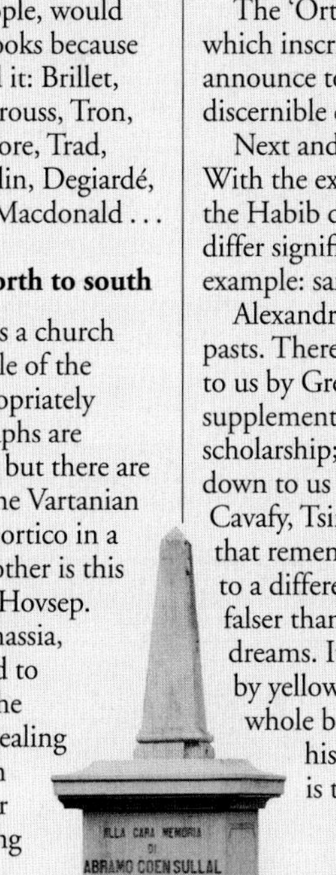

A monument in the Jewish cemetery.

THE BIBLIOTHECA ALEXANDRINA

The Bibliotheca Alexandrina is the brainchild of two academics at the University of Alexandria, who in 1974 came up with the idea of building a new library as a means of revitalizing their city. Sheer tenacity on their part gradually won over the authorities, and UNESCO gave the project its support. In 1988, the first stone was laid; in 1989, the Norwegian architectural firm Snohetta won an international competition with a highly original design; and in 1990 a founders' conference held in Aswan brought together all the leading players. A total of $65 million was raised, with the Gulf States and Iraq among the most generous donors.

The building occupies the site of the palaces of the Ptolemies, not far from the spot where the Great Library stood in antiquity. The link with the past is continually stressed, occasionally with a curious twist, since the Bibliotheca is sometimes referred to in official statements as a 'new beacon of knowledge', as though in punning allusion to the Pharos.

The design is exceptional both for its scale and for its bold aesthetic *parti*. A circular structure, 502 metres (1,647 feet) in circumference and going down 12 metres (40 feet) below the level of the neighbouring sea, it evokes the rising sun. On the surrounding grey granite surface, throughout the day, the sun spotlights incised letters in scripts from all over the world. Inside, there is a single vast reading room lit by indirect natural light, with views out over the Mediterranean, in which six hundred concrete columns rise up to flaring capitals in a way that recalls the papyriform columns of ancient Egyptian temples.

The collections are as yet far from complete: some 250,000 volumes have been acquired since 1990, but there is capacity ultimately for 8 million books. A further feature is a display of fine Arabic manuscripts borrowed from libraries in Alexandria, and of archival material from collections such as that of the Suez Canal Company.

Within the same complex are a planetarium, a science museum, and a museum of antiquities (with objects brought from other Egyptian museums, and the magnificent mosaics discovered during excavations carried out when the foundations of the new complex were being dug). There is also talk of setting up outside the Bibliotheca the colossal granite statue of a Ptolemy found at the site below Fort Qaitbay, on the other side of the bay, where the Pharos once stood.

The Bibliotheca Alexandrina enjoys the patronage of the President's wife, Madame Mubarak. In the capable hands of Sagag El-Dine (former vice-president of the World Bank), there can be no doubt that the project will prosper, providing a precious new resource for Alexandria.

Jean-Yves Empereur

FURTHER READING

HISTORY

David, Rosalie, *Discovering Ancient Egypt*, 1993
Hammond, N. G. L., and H. H. Scullard, eds *The Oxford Classical Dictionary*, 1970
Manley, Bill, *The Penguin Historical Atlas of Ancient Egypt*, 1996
Mansfield, Peter, *The British in Egypt*, 1971
—*The Arabs*, 1980
Moorhead, Alan, *The Blue Nile*, 1962
Norwich, John Julius, *Byzantium. The Early Centuries*, 1988
Richardson, Dan, *Egypt. The Rough Guide*, 1996
Runciman, Steven, *A History of the Crusades*, 1978
Woodward, Peter, *Nasser*, 1992

LITERATURE

Al-Kharrat, Edwar, *City of Saffron*, trans. Frances Liardet, 1989
C. P. Cavafy, *Collected Poems. C. P. Cavafy*, trans. Edmund Keeley and Philip Sherrard, 1975
Durrell, Lawrence, *The Alexandria Quartet*, 1962
—*Collected Poems 1931–1974*, 1980
Flaubert, Gustave, *The Letters of Gustave Flaubert, 1830–1857*, trans. Francis Steegmuller, 1981
Forster, E. M., *Alexandria, A History and a Guide*, 1922, 1982
—*Pharos and Pharillon, An Evocation of Alexandria,* 1923, 1983
Ibn Battuta, *Travels in Asia and Africa. 1325–1354*, trans. H. A. R. Gibb, 1983
Keeley, Edmund, *Cavafy's Alexandria*, 1996
Kennedy, Douglas, *Beyond the Pyramids*, 1989

Liddell, Robert, *Unreal City*, 1993
Mahfouz, Naguib, *Miramar*, trans. Fatima Moussa Mahmoud, 1993
Plutarch, *Plutarch's Life of Alexander*, trans. Sir Thomas North, 1911
Pye-Smith, Charlie, *The Other Nile*, 1986
Steegmuller, Francis, trans. and ed., *Flaubert in Egypt, a sensibility on tour, a narrative drawn from Gustave Flaubert's travel notes & letters*, 1983
Strabo, *The Geography of Strabo*, trans. H. L. Jones, 1917–32
Tsirkas, Stratis, *Drifting Cities*, trans. Kay Cicellis, 1974
Ungaretti, Giuseppe, *Life of Man*. A version with introduction by Allen Mandelbaum, 1958
— *Selected Poems*, trans. Patrick Creagh, 1971

CINEMA

Chahine, Youssef
—*Alexandria Again and Forever*, 1990
—*Adieu Bonaparte*, 1985
—*Alexandria, Why?*, 1978

ARCHAEOLOGY

For an account of recent archaeological discoveries see *Études alexandrines* (5 vols to date), IFAO, Cairo, and the website www.cea.com.eg

LIST OF ILLUSTRATIONS

The following abbreviations have been used:
a above; ***b*** below; ***m*** middle; ***l*** left; ***r*** right;
GRMA Greco-Roman Museum, Alexandria;
BNF Bibliothèque Nationale de France, Paris;
CEA–CNRS Centre d'Études Alexandrines–Centre National de Recherches Scientifiques

COVER

OPENING

CHAPTER 1

CHAPTER 2

CHAPTER 3

CHAPTER 4

82–3 'View of the esplanade or grand square of the new port and of the Arab walls' from the *Description de l'Égypte*, series E.M., 1809
83a Henri Mulard. *Episode from the Expedition to Egypt: General Bonaparte presenting a Sword to the Military Commander Mohammed el-Koraim* (detail), shown at the Salon of 1808. Oil on canvas. Châteaux de Versailles et de Trianon
84a *The Savants of the Egyptian Commission.* Preparatory drawing for the *Description de l'Égypte.* BNF
84b Inscription on a fragment of the helm of the *Dauphin Royal/Orient.* Fort Qaitbay.
85 Philip James de Loutherbourg. *The Battle of Alexandria, 21 March 1801* (detail), 1802. Oil on canvas. Scottish National Portrait Gallery, Edinburgh
86 Nicolas-Jacques Conté. *View of the Fort of Alexandria* (detail), 1798–1801. Watercolour. Private collection
87 André Dutertre. *The Alexandrian Sailor*, 1798–1801. Watercolour. BNF
88 *Mohammed Ali receiving an Embassy in his Palace at Alexandria, 12 May 1839.* Lithograph after David Roberts from *Egypt and Nubia*. Stapelton collection
89a *The Harem of Mohammed Ali, Alexandria.* Aquatint by Weber after a daguerreotype made by Horace Vernet on 7 November 1839, from N. P. Lerebours, *Excursions daguerriennes*, vol. I, 1841
89b Pascal Coste. *Plan of the Lock at the Head of the Mahmoudiya Canal*, 1820. Bibliothèque Saint-Charles, Marseille
90a John Varley Jr. *On the Mahmoudiya Canal, Alexandria*, 1880. Oil on canvas. Private collection
90–91 Pascal Coste, *View of the Coast of Alexandria from the Old Port*, 1819. Pen and ink. Bibliothèque Saint-Charles, Marseille
91a Hammerschmidt. 'Egypt, View of the Port of Alexandria'. Albumen print mounted on card, *c.* 1870. Collection of the author
92a 'Celebration of the Feast of 15 August [the Assumption] in Alexandria (Egypt): Procession of the French Colony passing the Hotel Abbat on the Way to the Latin Church', from *L'Illustration*, no. 1232, 6 October 1866
92b, 93b Apartment buildings on the Corniche designed by Loria, 1920s
93a Place des Consuls. German engraving, 19th century. Collection of the author
94 'Alexandria – the English Caracol, Attarine [Headquarters of the British Garrison], and Rue Rosette'. Postcard, *c.* 1910–20. Collection of the author
95a 'Alexandria – Place des Consuls'. Postcard (detail), *c.* 1910–20. Collection of the author
95b 'Alexandria – Rue Chérif Pacha'. Postcard, *c.* 1910–20. Collection of the author
96al Advertisement for Dunlop tyres, from the 1934/5 yearbook and tourist guide of the Royal Automobile Club of Egypt. Private collection
96ar, 96b, 97a, 97 mr, 97b Publicity for the Dorès photographic studio, Coutarelli Frères cigarette manufacturers, Sednaoui & Co. stores, the jewellers Zivy Frères & Co., and the tailor Papazian, from the magazine *Alexandrie, reine de la Méditerranée*, no. 1, July 1928. Private collection
96–97m Business letters posted from Alexandria on 14 December 1920, 29 June 1925 and 24 May 1873. Collection of the author
98al Interior of the 'Averoffeio' Greek school for girls
98b Bathroom in the former residence of a royal princess. Royal Jewelry Museum, Alexandria
98ar, 99 Three interiors in the Villa Cordahi in Rushdy
100a 'Alexandria – the Exchange'. Postcard, *c.* 1910–20. Collection of the author
100b Jewish Free School, Fondation de Menasce, *c.* 1905. Collection Gholam-Milhem
101 'Alexandria – Rue Midan (Arab quarter)'. Postcard, *c.* 1910–20. Collection of the author
102a, 102b 'The English Consulate (ruins)' and 'The Rue de la Poste Italienne (ruins)'. Photographs by Luigi Fiorillo, 1882. Collection Mohamed Awad
103l Main facade of Fort Qaitbay, after 1882. Collection of the author
103r Execution during the 1881 riots in Alexandria. Photograph by Luigi Fiorillo(?). Albumen print mounted on card, published in Alain Fleig, *Rêves de papier, la photographie orientaliste, 1860–1914*, Ides et Calendes, 1997. Collection Alain Fleig
104a Facade of the Greco-Roman Museum. Postcard, *c.* 1910–20. Collection of the author
104b Detail of a letter from Heinrich Schliemann to the Papal Count Max de Zogheb, 4 January 1889. GRMA
105 Giuseppe Botti in the courtyard of a large tomb with Ionic peristyle in the Karmuz quarter of Alexandria. Late 19th century. GRMA
106l Mastheads of Alexandrian newspapers, from *La Réforme, 1895/1945*. Private collection
106r Title page of the Egyptian illustrated satirical magazine *Bourriquot*, 2 November 1895. Private collection

CHAPTER 5

DOCUMENTS

INDEX

Page numbers in *italics* refer to captions or marginal texts

A

B

C

D–E

F–G

H–L

M

N–P

Alexandria, from an 18th-century map

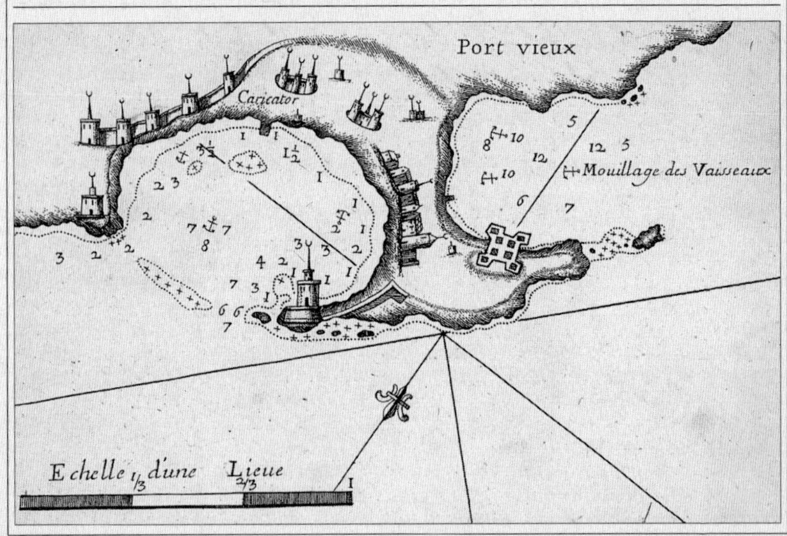

PHOTO CREDITS

AFP 118–20. AKG/W. Forman 30a, 46, 47, 48a. All rights reserved 63, 112b, 113, 149. American School of Classical Studies, Athens, Agora Excavations 39a. Artephot/R. Roland 37. Artephot/H. Stierlin 49. Austrian National Library, Vienna 35r. Awad Collection 102, 109. Bayerisches Staatsbibliothek, Munich 57. J. Bernard/Gallimard spine, 72a, 76b, 90–91, 137. Bibliothèque Nationale de France, Paris back cover, 36r, 39b, 43a, 64, 66b, 67b, 68–9, 70, 71a, 78b, 84a, 87, 129, 135. Bridgeman Giraudon 74, 85, 88. Bridgeman Giraudon/Christie's Images 90a. Bridgeman Giraudon/Dost Yayinlari 77. British Museum, London 66–7. J.-L. Bovot 54b. Cavafy Archives, Alexandria front cover inset, 108, 110b. CEA-CNRS front cover inset, 80, 91a, 93a, 94, 95, 96–7m, 100a, 101, 103l, 104, 105, 107a, 158. CEA-CNRS/J.-Y. Empereur 35l, 71b, 84b, 114. CEA-CNRS/J.-F. Gout 24, 26a, 31–3, 44a. CEA-CNRS/J.-C. Hurteau 27a, 76a, 78a. CEA-CNRS/A. Lecler 17, 23b, 24a, 26b, 27b, 28, 29, 30b, 34b, 56b, 73, 98–9, 125b. CEA-CNRS/A. Pelle 12, 15, 16b, 18, 25, 42, 44b, 48b, 52, 79a, 81, 92–3b, 123a. CEA-CNRS/C. Requi 23a. CEA/CNRS/G. Réveillac 60b. Peter Clayton, London 13. Collection Christophe L. 112a. Corbis/W. McNamee 122. G. Dagli Orti 55b, 58, 62. Philippe Delord 123b. Éditions Errance, Paris/J.-C. Golvin 14, 20–22, 36l. Éditions Ides et Calendes, Neuchâtel 103r. Éditions Parenthèses, Marseille 89b. Carlos Freire 1–9, 121, 127a. Gallimard Archives 72b, 79b, 82–3, 92a, 111b, 116a, 132, 133m, 133bl, 158. IMA, Paris/P. Maillard 65. IWM Photograph, London 117. Leemage/A. Jemolo 56a. Magnum/E. Lessing front cover inset, 61. Mémoires Juives-Patrimoine Photographique, Paris 100b. Musée Georges-Garret, Vesoul 18–19. Musée du Louvre, Paris/M. and P. Chuzeville 33b. Museum of Antiquities, Turin 45. Private collections 40b, 41b, 86, 96a, 96b, 97a, 97b, 106, 107b, 110a, 111a, 133a, 133br. RMN, Paris 50. RMN/Arnaudet 38. RMN/J. G. Berizzi 75. RMN/Chuzeville 60a. RMN/H. Lewandowski 40–41. RMN/R. G. Ojeda 82a. RMN/F. Raux 83a. Christian Richter front cover. Roger-Viollet 89a, 116b. J. Sassier/Éditions Gallimard 160. Scala 52–3, 54–5a. State Pushkin Museum of Fine Arts, Moscow 59. Technical Museum, Thessaloniki 43b. VT/Siny Most 34a. Witness/S. Compoint 11, 16a, 32, 51, 124–6, 127b, 128. www.saola.com/É. Brissaud 115.

TEXT CREDITS

Grateful acknowledgment is made for the use of material from the following works: (pp. 145–6) Edwar Al-Kharrat, *City of Saffron*, translated by Frances Liardet, Quartet Books Ltd, 1989; copyright © by Edwar Al-Kharrat 1986, translation copyright © by Frances Liardet 1989 • (pp. 140–41) Constantine Cavafy, 'Tomb of Iasis', 'The City', 'The God Abandons Antony', 'Days of 1909, '10, and '11', from *C. P. Cavafy: Collected Poems*, edited by Edmund Keeley and Philip Sherrard. Reprinted by permission of The Random House Group Ltd • (pp. 109, 143–4), Lawrence Durrell, *The Alexandria Quartet*, Faber and Faber Ltd, 1962; one-volume edition copyright © Lawrence Durrell 1962 • (p. 144) Lawrence Durrell, 'At Alexandria', *Collected Poems 1931–1974*, Faber and Faber Ltd, 1985; copyright © Lawrence Durrell 1957, 1960, 1968, 1971, 1977, 1980 • (p. 132) E. M. Forster, *Alexandria. A History and a Guide*. Edition with Afterword and Notes by Michael Haag, 1982; copyright © 1982 by Michael Haag Ltd • (pp. 108–9, 138). E. M. Forster, *Pharos and Pharillon*, 1923, Michael Haag Limited, 1983; copyright © 1951 E. M. Forster; renewal copyright © 1979 The Provost and Scholars of King's College, Cambridge • (inside front cover, p. 145) Naguib Mahfouz, *Miramar*, translated by Fatma Moussa Mahmoud, Doubleday, Transworld Publishers Ltd, 1993; copyright © 1967 by Naguib Mahfouz; English-language translation copyright © 1978 by The American University in Cairo Press • (pp. 142–3) Stratis Tsirkas, *Drifting Cities*, translation by Kay Cicellis, 1974; copyright © 1960, 1962, 1965, by Stratis Tsirkas, translation copyright © 1974 by Alfred A. Knopf, Inc. • (pp. 141–2) Giuseppe Ungaretti, 'Levant', 'Silence', copyright © Arnoldo Mondadori Editore, 1969; translations copyright © Patrick Creagh, 1971.

ACKNOWLEDGMENTS

The author and publishers wish to thank Claudio Gallazzi for the papyri on pp. 40–41, Louis Adem for material on 'Cosmopolitan Alexandria', Mohamed Awad for the photographs of the 1882 bombardment and especially for the portrait of Lawrence Durrell by Clea Badaro, and Lucien Basch for his text on the Latin cemeteries. The statistics in Chapter 4 are drawn from Robert Ilbert's *Alexandrie 1830–1930*.

Jean-Yves Empereur
is a classical scholar and archaeologist.
As first a member and then secretary-general of the French School of Archaeology in Athens, over a period of twelve years he studied the inscriptions at Delphi and carried out excavations at Argos, Delos and Thasos, where he began the underwater exploration of the ancient port. He also led investigations of the port of Amathus in Cyprus and of an ancient potters' village at Cnidos in Turkey. In 1990 he founded the Centre d'Études Alexandrines. The Centre has been responsible for some dozen excavations since 1992, of which the most recent are those of the Pharos, of wrecks off Fort Qaitbay, and of the Necropolis.

In memory
of Pierre Bruno, diver and friend

Translated from the French by Jane Brenton

First published in the United Kingdom in 2002 by
Thames & Hudson Ltd, 181A High Holborn,
London WC1V 7QX

www. thamesandhudson. com

British Library Cataloguing-in-Publication Data

A catalogue record for this book is available
from the British Library

ISBN 0–500–30110–7

Printed and bound in Italy
by Editoriale Lloyd, Trieste